*A
harvest
of ideas
for shooting
wonderful
color films
with any kind of
home movie
camera*

How to make GOOD

HOME

MOVIES

*by the
editors of
Eastman Kodak
Company*

*©1958 by the Eastman Kodak Company, Rochester, New York, U.S.A.
Printed and manufactured in the United States of America.*

PART ONE   *the essentials of movie-making*

Contents

Anything
is more fun
if you
start out with a bang!

• And if you have a choice, why not do it that way? After all, is there anyone who hates success? As Sophie Tucker once remarked, "I've been rich and I've been poor, but believe me, rich is better."

So, *How To Make Good Home Movies* is organized as two separate books in one. The first offers the quick and easy way. It encompasses the very least amount of information anyone would need to compile a good movie, not every possible kind of movie but the kind that beginners almost always start with and that most people shoot most of the time.

Part One isn't cluttered with unnecessary technicalities or with data that relates only to specialized types of movie making. After all, if you want to film some kids playing touch football on a bright sunny day, who cares *why* the correct lens setting is numbered 8, just as long as you know that 8 is the correct setting. In Part One the list of basic "things to remember" is trimmed to a manageable minimum. Once you've read it and go out to shoot a movie, you won't find yourself feeling like an apprentice juggler who has too many balls in the air.

Part Two covers the why's and wherefore's. It explains the reasoning behind most of the ideas you're asked to accept outright in Part One. But it includes much more. In it are relatively advanced movie making techniques, such as editing; it describes how to shoot movies in a wide range of unusual conditions and situations; it contains a collection of ideas you may wish to try as you become more experienced and confident.

The intent of this book, then, is to help you start at the top and then keep going up.

Chances are that you'll find one word used repeatedly on these pages in a way that doesn't jibe with your usual concept of it. This word is "scene." In a play or a commercial movie, a scene is a chain of action that occurs continuously in the same place at the same time. In talking about home movies though, it's more convenient to apply the term "scene" to the individual slice of action pictured each time you press and release the camera button. On a 50-foot roll of 8mm film, most people average about 24 home movie scenes (as the word is used in this book), but, if all of them show a baby being fed a single meal, the sum total might be only one scene of the other kind.

Chapter 1

Movies
are different
from
still pictures

Movies Show Actual Motion

The mantle of "World's Fastest Human" usually falls on an athlete who runs the 100-yard dash in a shade more than nine seconds. But if a normal boy or girl hangs his dungarees at your house, you may have a different candidate for the title. Most kids seem capable of turning in three laps around the living room in 0.0 seconds flat, with time included to upset a table lamp or a crystal vase.

Children move. Adults move, too, although generally at a less headlong pace. In this highly kinetic world of ours, nearly everything moves, and the recording of movement is a movie camera's chief *raison d'etre*.

Give a child a pogo stick, a snow shovel, a bicycle, or a cocker spaniel, and your snapshot camera will be able to freeze engaging and appealing slices of the reaction that occurs. With a movie camera, though, you can preserve the entire event, unfrozen and continuous, exactly as it happens.

Stiffly posing subjects, with or without feathered headress, belong in front of cigar stores, not movie cameras.

Stressing the fact that movies move may seem rather like pointing out that London is full of Englishmen; yet, owners of home movie equipment often transfer into their movie making unnecessary habits acquired in regular snapshooting. The most unnecessary is the concept of "hold it." To your movie camera it doesn't make the slightest difference whether the small boy in front of its lens is stiffened into the pose of a Grenadier Guardsman or whether he's hopping around like a kangaroo. It *should* make a difference to you, though. Almost any still camera, even the least costly, can produce a bigger and often a better picture of something that will stay put than a movie camera. When you bought your movie camera, you were mostly purchasing its ability to record continuous action in full color, and if you use it consistently for less than this, you simply are not getting 100 percent value from your investment.

Movies are best and most interesting when they show people actually doing things rather than merely smiling or waving tamely at the camera. A baby's first awkward steps, your family's vacation activities, a friend on water skis—these are the kinds of subjects that make memorable movies.

Of course, not every scene you shoot can be brimming with motion. Some of the larger works of man and nature simply won't co-operate. But, whenever you place eye to viewfinder, if you think primarily in terms of recording natural, interesting activity, your films will become a marvelously rewarding, continuing source of deep pleasure.

8

Movies Can Provide a Connected Story

The individual movie scenes you shoot are as intimately connected as Siamese twins simply because they are attached and follow one another along to the end of the reel. This provides them with a marvelous talent for telling a story.

"Story," at least as we use the term here, doesn't imply the scenario-plus-direction kind of production on display at your local theater or more local TV set. What it does imply is that normal activity, the kind most people like to see in their home movies, proceeds in a natural, logical sequence which usually explains itself, and that a movie containing scenes taken during such activity just naturally tells a story.

For example, when a very small boy receives his first snow shovel, he's more than likely to go through a number of separate actions. To start, of course, he'll take it from the person who's bought it for him, probably with a good deal of delight. Then, carrying it over his shoulder, he'll tramp out into the snow looking for a good place to start shoveling. He'll experiment with it, probably discover that certain loads are beyond his capacity, and finally become a pretty proficient snow shoveler. In the course of all this, he's played out a natural, everyday, typical small boy story, admittedly a simple one, but a story nevertheless. If you've merely followed along with your movie camera, shooting a little of each chapter, varying the length of your scenes and your shooting distance, you'll find, much to your pleasure, that you've captured a wonderful slice of childhood, complete and continuous, in a way that will make it repeatedly enjoyable not only to you, yourself, but to the audiences of friends and relatives who'll also see it.

When you bathe a small boy, there's sure to be a natural story . . .

9

. . . and your movie camera will find one in almost any normal activity.

This story-telling talent of home movies isn't, by any means, an automatic feature. Unless you make some effort to take advantage of it, your reels can be little more than a string of moving snapshots, with nothing tying them together but their physical connection. If you produce the kind of films that switch abruptly from a shot of the baby crawling, to one of Dad washing his new car, to one of Mom pruning a shrub, back to the baby eating a handful of dirt, you're missing one of the nicest, most unique advantages of home movies.

Movies Are Inexpensive

In terms of what you get for what you pay, a color movie on Kodachrome Film turns out to be a remarkably economical form of picturetaking. The 50-foot reel of 8mm film that comes back to you from the processing laboratory will provide your screen with four minutes of wonderfully lively action. Most moviemakers will break that four minutes up into approximately 24 separate scenes, each averaging 10 seconds in duration. If your camera is the type that takes its 8mm film in roll form, each of those 24 scenes will cost you about as much as one-and-a-half ordinary black-and-white snapshot prints; if you buy your film in the slightly more expensive magazine loads, the cost per Kodachrome scene will about equal that of two black-and-white prints.

A 50-foot roll or magazine of 16mm Kodachrome Film will project for about two minutes and contain, on the average, about a dozen scenes. The cost per 16mm scene is just about the same as that of shooting either a Kodacolor snapshot negative or a Kodachrome slide and having a color print made.

Chapter II

8 Tips
for
getting started
quickly

Load Your Camera in the Shade

This is especially important if it's a roll film type. The same bright light that creates a movie when it reaches the film through the camera lens can spoil a movie if it sneaks into the film during loading or unloading. Always keep one finger over the film on the full reel to prevent any accidental unwinding and, when you slip the end of the film into the slot on the empty reel, be sure to wind two turns of film around the core so that it will be securely fastened. Since the outer layers of film on each roll are there solely to protect the rest of the film from light during loading, check your camera manual to find out how this extra film should be run off before you begin actual movie making. And remember that a roll or magazine of 8mm film should go through the camera twice. After the first run, remove it, turn it over, reload, and shoot more movies. *(More detailed information on loading appears on page 85.)*

Keeping your index finger over the edge of the reel throughout loading insures that no film will be light-struck.

For Outdoor Movies Use Kodachrome Film, Daylight Type

Daylight and the light from the photoflood lamps you'll use for most indoor movies are not the same color. Daylight is quite a bit bluer and photoflood illumination is comparatively yellow. Since Kodachrome Film, Type A, is manufactured to provide natural looking colors under photoflood lighting, it will produce movies that are distressingly blue when used outdoors without a special colored filter over the camera lens. *(More data about films, including information about how one kind of film* can *be used both indoors and out is on page 88.)*

Shoot in Bright Sunlight with the Lens Opening Set at 8

The naturalness of the colors in your movies depends upon whether you use the correct lens opening for the light by which you are shooting. Make your first couple of movies in bright sunlight, since this is an easily recognizable kind of light and since it gives you colors at their most brilliant. The recommended lens setting for Kodachrome Film, Daylight Type, under bright sun (except in light-colored places, such as on beaches or snow) is $f/8$, or just plain 8. As long as you avoid photographing anything in shade, you'll produce wonderfully colorful movies from the start. *(To find out what settings to use in other kinds of daylight and just what to do in sandy or snowy conditions, see page 90.)*

Bright sunlight can be recognized from the dark shadows that accompany it.

Hold the Camera Close to Your Eye

If it is not close enough so that your eye can see the entire area of the viewfinder frame, your subjects will appear much farther away in your movies than you intended them to be. On some cameras which are capable of using more than one lens, the viewfinder will be marked off into three rectangles, one inside

What looks like this . . .

Unless your eye is right against the viewfinder, everything in your movie will be smaller and farther away than you intended.

. . . turns out like this.

the other. The middle-size rectangle (on the Brownie Movie Camera, Turret Model, it is printed in red) will show you what area is being reproduced on the film when you use the regular lens. The largest rectangle is for the wide-angle lens; the smallest, for the telephoto. If your viewfinder adjusts for different kinds of lenses, be sure it is set at the focal length (marked on the front of the lens in *mm*) of the lens actually on the camera. *(Viewfinding is discussed at greater length on page 96.)*

Wind the Camera After Each Scene

This insures that the camera's spring motor won't ever run down in the midst of some important moviemaking. A full winding keeps different cameras going for varying periods of time. On a Brownie Movie Camera, it will provide 48 seconds of shooting; on the Kodak K-100 Camera, 96 seconds. Although each is much longer than the average home movie scene of 10 to 12 seconds, few cameras have any device that tells you the amount of shooting time remaining. Only by habitually rewinding whenever you finish a scene, can you always be certain of completing whatever you start to photograph. *(There's more about winding on page 97.)*

To keep your camera steady, hold it firmly under the front with one hand, at the back with the other, and against your cheek.

See Your Instruction Booklet for the Correct Way to Hold Your Camera

Different movie cameras, like different lodges, require different grips. Unless the camera is firmly and comfortably nestled in your hands, your movies may look as if they had been shot from a storm-tossed rowboat. For additional steadiness, hold your arms close to your body, with the elbows pointed straight down. To follow skiing, running, boating, or similar action, simply keep the moving subject centered in your viewfinder and pivot smoothly at the waist. But be extremely cautious about moving your camera while shooting. Action should be from the subject, not from the camera. When you wish to show something too large for a single shot, aim at one side of it, start filming, and, after 2 or 3 seconds, begin pivoting very, *very,* VERY gradually at the waist until the viewfinder has reached the other side and then hold it there a few seconds. And never aim the camera vertically—that is, unless you're prepared to view your projected films from a recumbent position. *(For more about camera handling, turn to page 98.)*

Focus the Lens of Your 8mm Camera at 6 Feet

At the lens setting 8 (*f*/8) used with Kodachrome Film, Daylight Type, under bright sunlight, this will permit you to make a sharp picture of anything from 3½ feet to as far away as you can see. If the regular lens (it will be marked either 12mm or 13mm) on your 8mm camera is prefocused (e.g., you don't have to set it manually), this same approximate range of sharpness applies at a setting of 8. The range of sharpness is not quite as great with a 16mm camera. A regular (25mm) lens focused at 12 feet will place everything from 6 feet to as far away as you can see (infinity, marked ∞ on your camera) in sharp focus. *(Greater detail on focus hocus-pocus will be found on page 99.)*

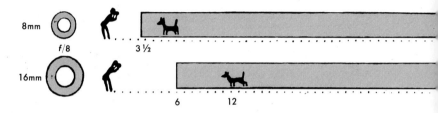

8mm

f/8　　3½

16mm

6　　12

Set the Camera for 16 Frames Per Second

When the film is moving through your camera so that 16 individual pictures (called "frames") are being exposed every second, the action in your movie will proceed at about the same pace it originally had as long as the projector is also set at the same speed. Most silent projectors are. Many 8mm and 16mm cameras do not have any adjustment of this sort, but are pre-set at 16 frames per second. If the film goes through the camera any more slowly, say at either 8 or 12 frames per second, movement in your movie will seem faster and choppier than normal; when the film goes through more quickly, say at 32 or 64 frames per second, the action is stretched out into the slow motion effect often employed in sports movies. *(Camera speeds are treated more exhaustively on page 102.)*

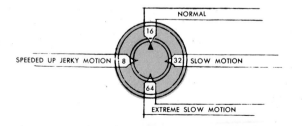

NORMAL

16

SPEEDED UP JERKY MOTION　8　　32　SLOW MOTION

64

EXTREME SLOW MOTION

15

Chapter III

Making an outdoor movie

Start with color, add plenty of action, and, chances are, you'll have a good movie. A low camera angle here helped emphasize both.

Getting Started the Easy Way

You've probably already equipped yourself, courtesy of the previous chapter, with a brief mental check list for simplified outdoor moviemaking.

- bright sunlight
- camera loaded with Kodachrome Film, Daylight Type
- lens set at 8
- focus at 6 feet for 8mm cameras, 12 feet for 16mm
- camera speed at 16 frames per second

All to the good. But items like correct exposure and sharp focus are only mechanical factors, certainly important, but still purely mechanical. The most accurately exposed home movie ever made might also be the dullest. The vital ingredients for a good film are the action occurring in front of the camera and the thought processes occurring behind it.

17

Few people enter upon home movie shooting out of any fatal fascination with the photographic details of it. Usually the impetus is the simple desire to preserve things — perhaps the pageant of a vacation trip or the doings of a growing family. Most of us want good movies, but we want to achieve them without the fuss that would make our camera a constant and annoying preoccupation. The question, though, is "How?"

Knowing a little about shooting good movies really starts with knowing a little about people and the way they react to the presence of any device photographic. To only the most youthful or the most misanthropic, is a camera inconsequential. When most others become aware that a camera's unblinking stare is aimed in their direction, they react stiffly, self-consciously, and inhibitedly. To capture them unself-conscious and relatively uninhibited, your best bet is to plan your shooting for occasions when your intended subjects are engrossed in some sort of activity.

This offers two advantages of no mean proportion. First, a person who's interested in whatever he's doing isn't likely to be bothered much by a camera. In addition, natural activities imply some sort of natural story pattern, and a story, no matter how rudimentary, is a tremendous asset to any movie.

So, before you start to shoot, think. Instead of simply deciding point blank to make a movie of your family, for example, hold your fire until they are engaged in some movie-worthy activity. If one doesn't begin spontaneously, launch it yourself.

Putting a Movie Together

Let's say you've picked up a roll of film that you'd like to use during the weekend. You know some friends are due over for an afternoon cookout. Save your film for this. Here's how you might make such a movie without your becoming a nuisance to the rest of the group and without the camera's becoming a nuisance to you.

A good story starts by setting the scene, so you could first shoot an over-all view of your back yard and house, preferably with some member of your family working around it, as someone undoubtedly would be, getting ready for the cookout. This immediately establishes where the action is going to take place and need consume only about 6 to 10 seconds. You might then move in for a closer shot to show exactly what kind of work the person is doing, whether it be setting up the table or dumping charcoal into the grill.

When your guests arrive, perhaps toting the dessert or some other contribution, you might try shooting some footage of

A country fair? Take your camera. And for a colorful finale, the hustling trotters and silks of their drivers.

Whenever your movie camera accompanies you to any sort of special event, even one that generates as much tension as a sports car race, be sure to aim it occasionally at some of the sidelights. Scenes of the careening cars will seem even more exciting when interspersed with brief views of the anxious pit crews and the spectators.

them without tipping them off, but there's always a chance that the first awareness of the camera might cause them to freeze in their tracks and merely gape at it. This is one type of shot that is often better if "semi-acted" rather than photographed impromptu.

Eventually, someone will light the fire (a good spot for a brief, very close close-up showing just hands, match, and charcoal) and then, more than likely, the chef will make his entrance, perhaps in the uniform of his calling and carrying a platter of succulent steaks — or are they hamburgers? Whatever the fare may be, when he places the meat on the grill, bring the camera close enough so it can really see what he's about and then move it much, much closer for a view of the red, marbled steaks (or hamburgers) sizzling over the fire or being turned.

21

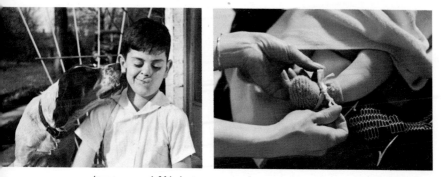

At a range of 3½ feet, your movie camera covers an area of about this size. You can exploit its close-up shooting ability by closing in on faces or filling the screen with important details.

This, again, might be only a brief scene but will add variety and help tie the story together. Close-ups of this sort and of people are the true spice of home moviemaking, the element that gives it a unique visual impact. Perhaps the greatest fault in most home movies is that they lack sufficient close-ups. Even with inexpensive, nonfocusing equipment, such as a Brownie Movie Camera, you can get sharp movies from as near as 3½ feet on a bright sunny day. At this range the camera eye takes in an area only about 10 by 15 inches.

Once the food is served, detach yourself momentarily from your own plate for a scene or two of the entire group at the table. If you'd like, you can even get into the picture yourself. Most cameras have a lock adjustment on the camera button which will keep the camera running without a finger actually pressed over the button. Just set the camera on some firm support — a table or chair will do if you don't have a tripod — aim it, lock the button, and join the rest of the party. After a few seconds, get up, walk outside the area covered by the camera lens, approach the camera, and release the button.

Eating time is also a good time for close-ups of each person at the table, especially the kids if there are any. It's always fun to see a small girl tackling a large hot dog or an eager boy burrowing into an over-sized slice of watermelon.

On most cameras the button can be locked in the "on" position, enabling you to get in the picture, by pressing it a notch farther than normal.

Whatever the program after dinner, whether it's merely sitting around companionably over a tall drink or working off the effects of overeating with a bit of croquet, badminton, or softball, it, too, belongs in your movie.

By the time your guests leave or it simply has become too late in the day for good color shots of people (usually a couple of hours before sunset), you'll have collected much more than a mere hodgepodge of isolated moving snapshots. Inside your camera, imprisoned on the film and ready for processing, is a truly documentary film story of the cookout, just as it happened. If you've remembered to vary camera-to-subject distances and scene lengths, and to include an ample sampling of close-ups, it's certain to be a continuing source of pleasure for many years to come.

Variety and Accurate Exposure

Of course, this isn't a formula for making a movie of a picnic or cookout. It's simply an example of the kind of scenes that will add up to a good film and how they can be put together so as to have an interesting continuity.

Both scene length and subject distance are topics that come in for a more exhaustive treatment in Chapter IX (page 104), but the central point about both is that they should be varied

WAR IN THE SNOW

Anyone can make a movie of a gang of boys standing around and looking uncomfortable. Chances are that confronted by a movie camera this is just about what most boys would normally do. But if in the midst of some activity of their own choosing or one you've prodded them into for your own devious purposes—a snowball fight, for instance—they probably won't be inhibited by the camera and may add a little extra enthusiasm to their efforts, hams that they are. It's important, though, to keep the camera on the sidelines. In a snowball fight, of course, you may be klonked on the back of the head if you don't. But in anything going along under its own steam, if you intrude too much or try to direct too much, it's likely to lose all of its genuine flavor and the result won't have the really memorable quality that spells out "B-O-Y."

When our boys pack up for a war in the snow, they equip for a major engineering project.

Of course, Steve and John are willing to let Gerry do the heavy labor, as long as he insists.

24

Since Tom is the architect of the defensive works, he gets to lay the cornerstone.

That's Gerry smoothing down the frontal armor plate, with his brother Hank in the background.

By now the fort is beginning to take on a fairly formidable appearance . . .

. . . although it's not nearly as high as desired, . . .

. . . especially by Tom, who'll settle for nothing less than complete protection.

Finally it's time to stock up the defender's armory . . .

25

Continued on page 28

from one scene to another whenever possible. Some activities deserve 15 seconds of camera time, while others can be covered neatly in 5. It's hardly ever necessary to shoot a single burst much longer than 15 seconds in duration. Instead, cover a continuous activity in brief scenes made from several different distances and angles. This not only economizes on film but produces a livelier, less static movie.

It's quite desirable to make your first few outdoor movies in bright sunshine, not only because it produces bright colors but because it is a lighting condition extremely easy to identify. Often, though, an event or a good movie opportunity will occur in other than bright sun and can't be postponed. To shoot movies under other classifications of daylight, it's only necessary to use a lens setting different from 8. These classifications are defined on page 91. The settings recommended for them with Kodachrome Film, Daylight Type, are also shown on the same page. For a handy, pocket-sized reminder of them, ask your camera dealer for a *Kodak Movie Dial,* which also contains a great deal of other useful information.

The Kodak Movie Dial actually consists of two dials, one giving lens settings for outdoor movie making under different kinds of sunlight and the other, settings for indoor movies made with photoflood lamps mounted on a photo light bar.

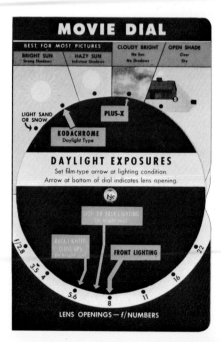

In bright sun, subjects containing large areas of light sand or snow and without people in the close foreground should be photographed with the lens set at 11 rather than 8. Scenes of water, when the surface is glaring, should also be exposed at a setting of 11.

The only important adjustment you need make for bright sunshine shooting occurs when you are photographing scenery that doesn't include nearby people but does contain large areas of light sand or snow. The setting for this special kind of subject should be 11.

Remember that the movies you'll want to have tomorrow must be shot today. So, in addition to using your camera on the special occasions that suggest moviemaking almost automatically — the weddings, the vacations, the parties, and the holidays — keep it busy on some of the more commonplace but, in retrospect, equally memorable ones. Take it with you on visits to the zoo, to fairs, and to amusement parks; photograph the kids learning to ride their bikes and to roller skate; shoot movies of your boating, swimming, fishing, and golfing activities; use it whenever you go visiting or even fly a kite. As long as something's going on, there's a good potential movie.

27

Continued from page 25

... and Tom figures on pro-
longed hostilities.

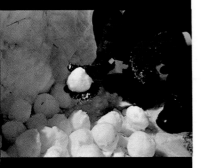

Charge!

Hank and Steve get ready . . .

... and let go with a barrage.

But Tom has a small barrage of
his own ready to launch . . .

... and Steve receives a direct hit.

As with most fortifications, one dent generally . . .

. . . leads to others . . .

. . . and although the defensive troops still have plenty of fight left in them, . . .

. . . as Steve can testify (that Steve, he always gets it), . . .

. . . the victors really rub it in with a vengeance.

And that, as Tom and Gerry are willing to admit, is that.

29

Making
a Snowman

A DOG
GETS A BATH

LEARNING
TO
WATER SKI

A DAY OF
SWIMMING

TWO KIDS,
ONE
SAND BOX

A Few Examples

The ideas you'll find here aren't meant as scripts. Most really good home movies aren't the fruit of scripts anyway, but rather of things photographed as they happened and logically linked together. These ideas are simply examples of the kinds of scenes which would contribute to a pleasant movie record of the over-all activity during which they'd occurred. They certainly won't fit everyone or, perhaps, anyone. When your family goes to the beach it's possible that the youngest offspring, rather than needing any swimming instruction from you, may know and use more strokes than a duffer in a sand trap. But if none of these collections applies strictly to your own shooting, they may offer some ideas you'll find highly useful. For vacation films, you'll also find many helpful hints in the booklet, *Vacation USA With Your Color Camera,* available from many Kodak dealers.

Making a Snowman

- *The kids and one parent come trooping out into the park or onto the lawn*
- *The parent shows them how to roll the big snowballs needed for a snowman*
- *Close-up of a child's hands starting to roll a snowball*
- *The parent, with help from the kids, stacks the large snowballs to form the body and head*
- *Close-up of one of the kids making the face*
- *The arms are stuck into the body and someone adds a hat for a debonair touch*
- *The sculptors pose, probably mugging, with their work of art*

The Dog Gets a Bath

- *Close-up shows water from a garden hose being run into a large tub or child's wading pool*
- *Someone pours bubble bath into the water and stirs it up*
- *One of the family calls the dog and he comes bounding into view.*
- *Attempts are made to lure the dog into the bath*
- *He is finally dragged in bodily*
- *Medium-length and close-up shots of the dog undergoing his trial by soap and water*
- *Finally released from the bath, the dog is swabbed with towels*
- *He ends matters by shaking all over his bathers*

You can get good color movies even if your subject isn't
in the sun. For data on open
shade shooting, see page 91. ▶

A movie needn't show every
bit of an activity. Scenes of
the high spots tell the story. ⬇

A bucking horse spells "rodeo" better
than any view of a grandstand. A football scrimmage or "tractor driver"
spells "boy" as no tame version can.
Your movie camera delivers the greatest dividends when trained on action. ▶

Learning to Water Ski

- *Someone far out on the lake comes skiing toward the camera*
- *He comes in to shore, kicks off his skis, and talks some member of the family into trying it*
- *Medium-length and close-up shots show the neophyte receiving preliminary instructions*
- *The pupil puts on his skis, the boat pulls away, and, more than likely, he falls down*
- *After several other unsuccessful tries, he finally manages to stay on his feet*
- *The photographer gets into the boat and shoots some footage of the new water skier in action*
- *The boat pulls back into shore*
- *Close-up shows the new skier happily mopping himself off with a towel*

A Day of Swimming

- *The family loading the car with food, beach equipment, blankets*
- *Scenery along the way and the approaches to the lake or ocean can be shot directly through the front windshield while the car is moving*

- *The children running down the shore and splashing into the water*
- *Swimming instruction for the smallest child, with close-ups of the neophyte merman or mermaid*
- *Lunchtime*
- *Shots of the members of the family using floats or inflatable animals or engaged in water fights*
- *Special stunts, such as one of the kids diving off dad's shoulders*
- *Wet swimmers flinging themselves onto the blanket for a session of sun worship*
- *Packing up the equipment and reloading it into the car for the trip home*

Two Kids, One Sandbox

- *The children carrying pails, shovels, and other toys, coming out of the house or garage*
- *Making cakes, undertaking construction projects, and producing other creative achievements with close-ups of the handiwork*
- *Not-so-creative achievements, like shampooing each other's hair with sand*
- *Mother drags the kids out of the sandbox and performs on-the-spot cleanup*

Every trip to a photo-scenic locale isn't a honeymoon, but every sight-seeing film you shoot can take advantage of the ideas in this movie story (it has about as many scenes as you can get comfortably into a roll of 8mm film) for showing place, people at place, and ending up with a pleasant, natural narrative. The initial scene is an overall view of the American Falls. The next two show the bride getting a more intimate look. Then the camera peers down at the wooden catwalk of the Cave Of The Winds and, immediately after, you have the slightly damp couple trudging along that catwalk. Each time, the film displays the locale first, then the people in it. By the way, if you should want your entire party in some scenes as the couple is here, just set the camera and ask a friendly-looking bystander if he'll do the shooting. You'll hardly ever get a turn-down.

You just hear it first, but suddenly there it is, looking like every post-card of it you've ever seen.

Anne wanted the bird's-eye view, but you'll notice that she didn't let go of that railing.

She decided that the telescope was a safer way of getting a close look than going over in a barrel.

That spindly-looking structure down below is the catwalk at the Cave of the Winds.

It was with no few trepidations that we decided to try it out.

Actually it isn't as rickety as it looks—nothing could be.

When you see all that water, you feel a strong impulse to get back to solid ground.

Needless to say, despite the slickers, it gets dampish down there under the Falls.

37

Continued on page 40

A Parade

- *Shots of the crowd waiting along both sides of the street*
- *The vanguard of the parade moving toward your stationary camera*
- *Different elements of the parade, bands, floats, drill teams, as they go by — you can follow them by swinging around slowly with your camera, making the swivel from your waist*
- *Side action such as the expressions on children's faces, vendors selling balloons, food, and souvenirs — these scenes can be interspersed with scenes of the actual parade*
- *The last marching unit going by and the crowd streaming out into the street*

A Scenic Trip

- *Shoot through the window of your train, plane, or bus as it pulls away from your home departure point as long as it isn't shaded or indoors*
- *Get scenes of any interesting scenery you pass, shooting through the window or windshield of your plane, train, bus, or car*

- *Close-ups of signs describing any scenic attractions followed up by views of the attractions themselves*
- *Shoot extremely tall objects, such as skyscrapers, waterfalls, or sequoia trees by starting either at the top or bottom and then moving the camera very, very slowly toward the opposite extremity*
- *Get close-ups and medium-distance shots of members of your party engaged in characteristic activities, for example, riding burros down into Grand Canyon, feeding the pelicans at St. Petersburg, or buying souvenirs anywhere*
- *Include informal activities, such as picnics, swimming, feeding birds, and animals*

Review of Camera Settings

Lens opening: determines whether movies and their colors will be dark, natural-looking, or light; the numbers may have an f/ in front of them; they will usually be in a series like 1.9, 2.8, 4, 5.6, 8, 11, 16 although the first number might be 2.3 or 2.7; the smallest numbers are the largest openings.

Focus: determines whether the subject will appear sharp and distinct or fuzzy and indistinct; on many cameras it is pre-set for maximum range of sharpness; the settings will almost always be in terms of feet.

Camera speed: determines whether motion will be shown normally, slower than normal, or faster than normal; many cameras are pre-set at 16 frames per second, normal speed for silent movies; some cameras offer a choice of speeds, usually from among 8, 12, 32, 48, and 64 frames per second.

Continued from page 37

The border runs along the middle of the river and across the middle of the bridge . . .

. . . and so before you leave the span, you encounter Canadian Customs.

The Customs Officer sees so many honeymooners that he doesn't even crack jokes.

He cleared us politely and rapidly and sent us on our way.

After checking in at the hotel, we felt like taking a quick tour around the Canadian side.

We ran into a policeman . . .

. . . who suggested that we might be likely to enjoy . . .

. . . a ride in a surrey, complete with fringe and friendly driver.

Anne discussed routing with him and told him that all we wanted to see was everything.

He helped her in and away we clip-clopped.

A horsedrawn pace is ideal for viewing the Falls. It gives you time to gauge their size.

And anyway, someone's got to support the horse.

41

Chapter IV

Making
an
indoor movie

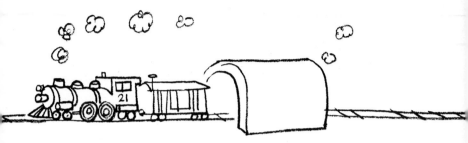

Indoor Movie Opportunities

Once there were a brother and sister, both of tender years, who, after a simply exhausting day of snacking on homemade mud pies, rolling in piles of grass clippings, and engaging in other delightful but equally grimy pastimes, were marched energetically into the bathroom for their communal scrubdown. Here they competed in brisk undressing contests, hurled themselves into the tub with great enthusiasm, shampooed each other with extremely soapy water, conducted boat races in which both cheated shamefully, and left their bespattered parents amused, exhausted, and totally unconscious that such carryings-on make wonderful home movies.

Unfortunately, many movie cameras lead a neglected indoor life because their owners aren't conscious of the opportunities for good movies that constantly surround them. Parents who faithfully chronicle the outdoor activities of their families often forget that much of a child's life occurs indoors, that birthdays are movie-worthy occasions, and that Christmas and other holidays inevitably sneak around every 365 days or so. Many people who wouldn't be parted from their movie cameras on a vacation trip somehow ignore them for weddings and parties. If it were more difficult or considerably more costly to shoot indoor movies, this might be understandable, but actually it's neither.

A movie camera outdoors is a relatively inconspicuous item. Indoors, though, its attendant photoflood lamps are a constant source of distraction to the people you photograph. For best results, they should be shown in some sort of interesting activities and encouraged to perform those activities as if the camera wasn't looking in.

There's at least one instance in which home movies have a certain advantage over the original event — aspiring young trumpet players are seen, but not heard.

Electrical Sunlight

In fact, there's really only one great difference between indoor and outdoor shooting, a difference pivoting on the kind of light employed. Outdoors there's hardly ever any shortage of sufficient moviemaking illumination, courtesy of the sun. Indoors, via our ordinary lighting facilities, there's usually enough for us to see what we're doing and to conduct the processes of life, but there isn't enough for shooting color movies.

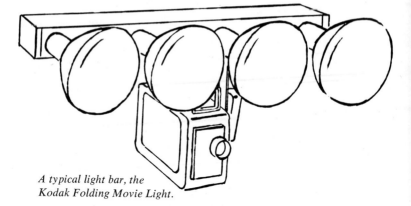

A typical light bar, the Kodak Folding Movie Light.

This shortcoming is remedied by an electrical device called a "movie light bar," a fixture that fastens to the bottom of your camera, contains sockets for either two or four photoflood lamps, and trails off a long cord that can be plugged into a convenient outlet. Click the light bar's switch, and everywhere you point your camera you also direct a strong beam of light.

Two photoflood lamps will doubtless seem extraordinarily brilliant to you, perhaps even more brilliant than the sun. The truth is that only at about arm's length will they be delivering as much light to your face as sunlight does on a bright day. At greater distances, the lamps bring considerably less light to the subject than a bright sun.

Setting The Lens Correctly

When shooting indoor movies with a photo light bar, the lens setting is governed by the distance from the lights to the subject. This is so because a subject near the lamps is more brightly illuminated than one far away. Outdoors, of course, the situation is entirely different. Whether you're in Alabama or Zanzibar, if there's a bright sun overhead and Kodachrome Film, Daylight Type, in your movie camera, the setting for an average subject will be 8. But this is so only because Alabama and Zanzibar are relatively about the same distance from the sun. If you happened to be running off a few feet of the same film

46

one bright sunny afternoon on the planet Jupiter, some four times farther from the sun than the Earth is, you'd need a much larger lens opening due to the fact that the sun's light is greatly diminished by the time it travels that extra distance.

If your subject is quite close, a large proportion of the illumination from your light bar will reach him and the lens opening can be a small one — a setting such as 5.6 or 8. When the subject is far away, though, relatively little light from the lamps will reach him so the lens opening must be a large one like 1.9 or 2.8. Printed directly on most photo light bars and also on the film instruction sheets is a table listing the correct settings to use at various shooting distances.

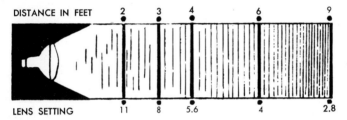

The farther a subject is from your lamps, the smaller the amount of light reaching him. These settings apply only with two lamps.

Of course, the more accurate your estimates of distance, the better your films will turn out, but this accuracy doesn't have to be of the tape measure kind. If your subject is 6 feet away and you guess either a foot too near or a foot too far, the error won't create a really significant loss of quality in your movie. One good means of gauging such distances is to imagine your own height laid out on the ground and measure mentally in terms of a half, one, one-and-a-half, or two body lengths.

CLOSING IN ON A BABY FACE

The expressions that wrinkle across a baby's face, from the stormiest to the sublimest, are all quite wonderful. Be sure to do much of your baby filming really close up, from 4 feet or nearer. If you give the baby time to become accustomed to the lights, chances are that they won't bother him.

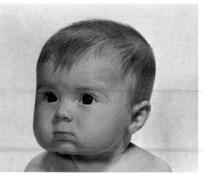

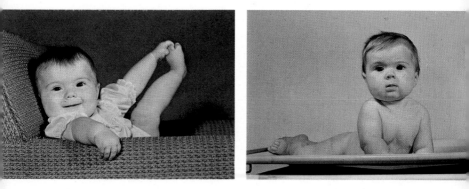

LENS SETTINGS FOR INDOOR MOVIES
Made with Photo Light Bar and Kodachrome Film, Type A

Distance in Feet	3	4	6	9	13
2 Lamps	8	5.6	4	2.7 or 2.8	1.9 or 2
4 Lamps	11	8	5.6	4	2.7 or 2.8

Lamps should be 375-Watt Medium Beam Reflector-Type Photofloods

Photoflood Lamps and Type A Film

Another important difference between real and electrical sunshine is their colors. Compared to actual sunlight, the illumination produced by photofloods is quite a bit more yellow-red in
tone. Photographers often describe it as "warmer." Since Kodachrome Film, Daylight Type, is made to produce natural-looking colors under the bluer, "cooler" daylight, it will cause
movies exposed on it by photofloods to appear unpleasant and
unnatural in over-all color. Kodachrome Film, Type A, however, is specially attuned to the kind of light produced by photoflood lamps and should always be used when shooting with a
light bar.

A package of Kodachrome Film, Type A, has boxes on the top and side with a large "A."

Not all photoflood lamps work well for movie shooting. Get 375-watt, medium-beam floods.

50

The most convenient lamps for indoor home moviemaking are 375-watt, medium-beam, reflector-type photofloods. These have reflectors built right into their globes, and two of them create a much greater total amount of light than all of the regular fixtures found in most rooms.* Four 375-watt lamps will double the light output of two, but more than four are usually unnecessary and may blow a fuse.

These lamps become progressively weaker as they burn. After one hour you should use a lens opening one-half setting *larger* than you'd need with new lamps. For example, if your lamps had been on for a total of more than an hour and you were at a distance for which the table suggested a setting of 5.6, you should actually set the lens halfway between 5.6 and 4. After two hours of lamp life, the compensation should be a full setting larger, or, in this example, 4.

The necessity of changing the lens setting every time you change the range between your camera and your subject provides an automatic means of gauging just how much variety you're working into your movie shooting. When you find yourself making frequent changes in lens setting, you can count on the fact that your results will be a lot more interesting to watch than a film shot with an unvarying camera to subject distance.

Photoflood lamps, while your staunchest ally for indoor moviemaking, are also likely to be one of your chief headaches, mostly because they call so much attention to the fact that movies are being shot and because, at close range, they are so dazzling. Their constant presence can inhibit even the most normally uninhibitable child. There's no pat solution to this difficulty but one means of easing the situation is to turn the lights on five or ten minutes before you actually plan to start shooting. Your prospective subjects can then become somewhat more accustomed to them than if they had to face them abruptly.

NOTE—The light from photoflood lamps will not harm any normal eyesight. Cold liquids will, however, cause these lamps to explode and should not be splashed anywhere in the vicinity of lighted or still hot lamps.

Ordinary household incandescent light bulbs provide light not only lacking in the brightness needed for color moviemaking, but far too yellowish in color.

There's no use ignoring the all-too-obvious fact that most adults feel somewhat ill at ease in the bright beam of a movie light bar. They're less uncomfortable, though, when doing something with a child and especially when in a completely relaxed situation, such as a party.

When boy meets bologna sandwich, especially small boy and large sandwich, the movie potentialities are measureless. Children at mealtime are always first-rate movie subjects and easy ones, chiefly because they stay put.

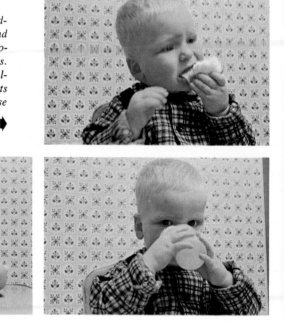

Getting Down to the Shooting

To see how all of this works in practice, let's say that some very young person in whom you have an interest is about to be fed his breakfast. Even before he's deposited in his high chair or at his feeder table, turn your photofloods on so that he'll become adjusted to their presence. Then, when his meal is ready, pick up your camera and step back far enough for an over-all view of his mother bibbing him and presenting him with his cereal.

53

The distance might be about 12 or 13 feet. Check the table on your light bar or on the Kodak Movie Dial, and it will report that for two lamps the lens setting should be 1.9 or 2. Focus, if your camera requires it, and shoot 8 to 10 seconds worth to launch the story. Then, move in closer, perhaps to 7 feet, so that you can catch his efforts to maneuver spoon into mouth. At 7 feet, the table will suggest a setting of 3.5 (or halfway between 2.8 and 4) for two lamps. After several bursts, during which your small subject probably coats his outside with as much cereal as he does his inside, you might move in to about 4 feet for a real close-up of his oatmeal-encrusted face. Here the setting would be 5.6.

Once you've become accustomed to changing openings every time you or your subject changes position, the rest of the routine for a good movie will be just as it was outdoors — shoot natural activity, vary distance and scene length frequently, include plenty of close-ups, and try to tell a story.

The only important booby-trap unique to indoor shooting is that extremely reflective, shiny surfaces can hurl big glare spots back into your lens. If a mirror or some other glossy surface is close behind your subject, always shoot from at least a 45-degree angle to this surface so that the reflection will be outside the picture area.

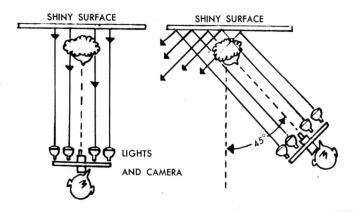

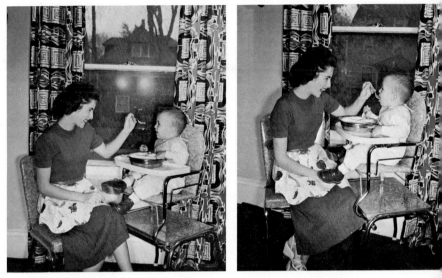

When the beams of your photoflood lamps are aimed directly into any highly reflective surface, the flaring reflection will spoil the entire movie scene. If there should be some glass or a similar material in the background of a scene, move your shooting position around to one side so that when you look through the camera finder, you don't see your own image or that of the lights.

A Few Examples

You may not have a batheable baby, an all-consuming passion for model trains, or the slightest desire to officiate at an adult party celebrating Halloween. Be that as it may, the ideas listed on pages 58 and 59 could help you acquire a better appreciation of how to assemble a good indoor movie reel about some subject in which you are interested. If you should be planning to capture on film your small one's next soap-and-water stint, your miniature "iron horse" in action, or a forthcoming Halloween divertissement, many of these suggested scenes may work out very nicely for you.

LAURA'S
SEVENTH
BIRTHDAY

Any movie of a birthday party could hardly avoid being a sheer delight, but if it starts with the party proper it may miss fully half of the fun. In the twenty scenes of this birthday story—a number of scenes, by the way, that you can easily make on a single roll of 8mm film—the first nine show the preparations for the party and only the last eleven the party itself. In shooting movies of other special events, you'll invariably find that the film will turn out to be more interesting if you do begin with the groundwork. At Thanksgiving, instead of making your first scenes at the dinner table, begin in the kitchen several hours earlier. At Christmas, rather than shooting the initial scenes on the morning of the twenty-fifth, devote a portion of your film to the trimming of the tree the night before.

56

Of course the invitations had gone out in the mail a week before, but Laura just had to double check.

Cake icing is always a source of great interest and, as usual, there was no dearth of help for Mother.

It was quite a race to see if Laura could ice the cake before sister Gail iced her stomach.

Spectator response became a shade apathetic at times, but . . .

. . . there was plenty of activity when it came time to stick the candles in.

Laura counted twice, just to make sure there were seven.

She also served as assistant interior decorator.

Heaven knows, a young lady has to look glamorous on her very own seventh birthday . . .

57

Continued on page 60

Baby Takes a Bath

- *Close-up of water being poured into the tub, dishpan, or bathinette*
- *Baby being lifted by its mother out of the crib or playpen*
- *Scenes, from varying distances and angles, of the baby being undressed*
- *Medium-distance scene of the baby being lowered gently into the water*
- *Close-up of the baby's face to catch his reaction*
- *Medium-distance scenes of the baby being washed and of him splashing and playing*
- *Baby being taken out of the water and wrapped in a towel*
- *Close-up of the baby's face while he is being dried and his hair combed*
- *Baby being dressed and then given his bottle*

Model Trains in Action

- *Close-up of an engine as smoke starts to puff out of its smoke-stack and it slowly begins to move forward*
- *Medium-distance scenes of the train running through the layout*
- *Close-ups of such accessory items as a crossing gate closing and then the train racing past*
- *Brief scene showing boy or man in engineer's cap operating the transformer and remote-control equipment*

- *Close-up of a tunnel, with the train suddenly bursting out of it*
- *Scenes of the train pulling into the freight yard*
- *Close-ups of special gadgets at work, such as automatic freight car loaders, crane cars, and coal loaders*
- *The human engineer finally stops the train and turns off all of his battery of electrical equipment*

A Halloween Party for Adults

- *Brief scenes of costumed guests being greeted at the door by the hostess or host*
- *Close-up of hand ladling a cup of cider or punch from bowl*
- *Guests sitting around drinking cider or punch*
- *Scenes of different guests struggling through games, with many close-ups of faces as people bob for apples, squirm under the barrier in low-crawling contest, or exhibit confusion while trying to pin-the-tail-on-the-donkey*
- *Over-all scene as some dancing commences*
- *Medium-distance scenes of people with incongruous or clumsy costumes trying to dance with each other*
- *Final scene of everyone in the kitchen for an impromptu snack*

Continued from page 57

. . . but this hundred strokes business is simply ridiculous.

But it all turned out to be very much worthwhile, . . .

. . . although it was sometimes hard to tell whose gifts they were supposed to be.

After a brief time out for a bit of girlish chit-chat, . . .

. . . Pin-The-Tail-On-The-Donkey became the chief attraction . . .

. . . with the usual rather low level of marksmanship.

The only way to stop a sudden outbreak of balloon batting was to announce cake and ice cream.

First, of course, there had to be a chorus of "Happy Birthday" . . .

. . . and the other usual formalities, such as cake cutting . . .

. . . and favor opening.

A good time was had by all.

Well, nearly all.

61

Chapter **V**

Indoor and Outdoor Scenes
on the same reel

One Film, One Filter, Two Kinds of Light

The light indoors is different from the light outdoors. Therefore, there seems to be, photographically, a wall between them. But movie subjects respect no such barriers. Take Christmas.

With a photo light bar and Type A film you show delighted children scampering to the foot of the family tree and stirring up a shower of torn gift wrappings as they unveil their Yuletide loot. Fine. But then they hurriedly dress and race outside to test the toys. There you stand with a partly exposed roll of Type A film in your camera, now the wrong kind of film, and you miss half the fun.

Actually this problem, seemingly insurmountable, isn't insurmountable at all. To Type A film, everything bathed in the comparatively yellowish light of photoflood lamps "looks" natural or, in other words, colors appear pretty much as we accept them. But, when Type A film views through the camera lens a scene illuminated by bluish daylight, all of the colors in that scene will "look" unnaturally blue.

63

Available, though, at quite modest cost (less than three dollars for most movie cameras) is a pinkish "monocle" of rather remarkable capabilities. When placed over the lens of your camera, this device, called the Kodak Daylight Filter for Kodak Type A Color Films (No. 85), makes it possible to shoot scenes in daylight and have them turn out just about indistinguishable from scenes made on Daylight Type Film.

If you make an indoor movie with photoflood lamps and Daylight Type film, all of the colors will turn out much more yellowish than normal.

When Kodachrome Film, Type A, is used outdoors without a filter, the results will look like this. All colors have a strong bluish cast.

The most important implication of this is that it permits you to mix outdoor and indoor scenes on a single roll of Kodachrome Film, Type A. The only strain on your memory will be the necessity of putting the filter in place whenever you head outdoors and of removing it before you begin shooting by photofloods. The same outdoor lens settings recommended for Daylight Type film apply to the Type A-filter combination.

Filters come in several different sizes; so, before running off to purchase one, consult your camera instruction booklet for the applicable filter series number. It will probably be either 4 or 5. Since a filter will not remain in front of your camera lens

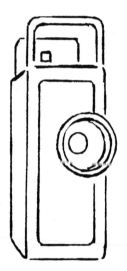

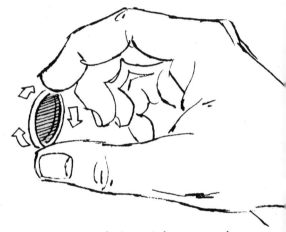

To switch from indoor to outdoor shooting with Type A film, place the Daylight Filter in the retaining ring and screw the ring into the lens mount.

65

by sheer determination, it's essential to have a retaining ring to hold it there. On many new cameras, these retaining rings are supplied as standard equipment, but if yours doesn't have one, your camera dealer can provide one at nominal cost.

For an introduction to more filters and more about filters, consult the section that begins on page 178.

For Magazine-Loading Cameras Only

This filter trick isn't, by any means, the only way of ending up with both indoor and outdoor action on the same reel. Magazine-loading movie cameras can do it in an entirely different manner, *sans* filter. Since the film for these cameras remains in a lighttight metal container until processing, there's no reason why a magazine of Daylight Type film shouldn't be replaced by one of Type A whenever the situation demands. To illustrate, there might be an afternoon birthday party at your house, one that begins indoors as the young guests arrive bearing gifts. You'd shoot this, of course, with a magazine of Type A film and your light bar. Then, when the kids troop outdoors for games, you need only remove the light bar and switch over to a magazine of Daylight Type film. When everyone swarms back inside for cake and ice cream, you'd merely put the original magazine of Type A film back into the camera, assuming you haven't exposed all of it, and return to your photofloods.

When your film is returned from processing, the complete story of the party will be rather disconnected because portions are on two different reels. Splicing these portions together into the correct sequence isn't difficult to do, but, of course, this additional step is eliminated entirely if you use the Type A-filter method instead.

If you should choose to alternate magazines of Daylight Type and Type A film in an 8mm magazine-loading camera, be sure to jot down on each magazine the exact reading of the camera's footage indicator when you remove it. Then, whenever you put that magazine back into the camera, you know where to reset the indicator and thus avoid any danger of losing part of your film. This procedure isn't necessary with 16mm magazines, since the footage remaining is indicated by the magazine itself.

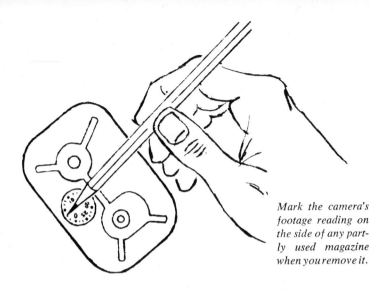

Mark the camera's footage reading on the side of any partly used magazine when you remove it.

Another Filter Alternative

The filter idea can be exploited with a reverse twist by loading Kodachrome Film, Daylight Type into your camera and slipping a Kodak Photoflood Filter for Kodak Daylight Type Color Films (No. 80B) over the lens when operating with your trusty light bar. While this works, it doesn't work especially well. First, the color rendition on indoor scenes isn't as good as that obtained with Type A film. Also, the filter prevents quite a bit of light—actually as much as a full half of it—from getting to the film. This is equivalent to having only one lamp on a two-lamp light bar actually contributing any light to your photographic efforts. It means that when you employ this filter you must use a lens opening one complete full setting *larger* than the one recommended for Type A film with photofloods. If the table on your light bar or instruction sheet should call for a setting of 5.6, you would have to use instead a lens setting of 4.

This last method, then, should be used only in emergency situations. Either of the others, however, will prove quite satisfactory, but, from the standpoint of convenience, Type A film with the Daylight Filter over the lens for outdoor shooting is certainly the most practical. Many moviemakers, even though they don't have both indoor and outdoor scenes on every reel they shoot, use it all the time simply because of its versatility.

getting
to the
ZOO

Almost every movie camera owner who also chances to be a parent is at some time beset by a suspicion that he hasn't made a reel of the children for an unwholesomely long time. So he buys film and if there isn't anything special going on, no birthdays or other childhood milestones, he wonders what in the world to do with it. Often, as demonstrated here, a very satisfactory answer is to devote that film to a normal Saturday or Sunday in the life of your small fry. Getting up, eating, bathing, going to the zoo may seem prosaic stuff, but the results will turn out surprisingly captivating. Especially here is it desirable to do all of the shooting on Type A film and use a Daylight Filter over the lens outdoors. Then, wherever the kids go and whenever they go, you and your camera can go along, too.

I like to greet the dawn as early as the next fellow, as long as the next fellow isn't my boy, Tommy.

He can be as persistent as a tax collector until he gets his glass of orange juice . . .

. . . and he gets every bit of it.

Meanwhile, another early riser is due for a little liquid refreshment, and small Douglas . . .

. . . doesn't mind it at all.

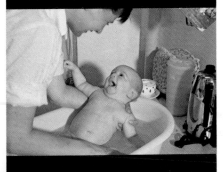

In fact, it's the getting out that he doesn't care for, . . .

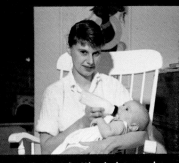

. . . but a bottle helps make him forget that.

It was much too nice out to stay indoors, so out we went . . .

Continued on page 72

A Few Examples

There probably are thousands of instances when better, more interesting movies would result from an ability to get both indoor and outdoor scenes on the same reel of film. Here are a very few. If you build model planes, go deer hunting, or have small children around at Christmas time, you may find some ideas that you can apply directly to your own shooting.

Test Flight

- *Close-up of the box in which the model plane kit was packaged*
- *Father and son with the completed subassemblies of the plane spread out on a worktable*
- *Medium-distance shots and close-ups of both of them completing the plane*
- *Close-up of son spinning the prop of the finished model*

ADD DAYLIGHT FILTER OR CHANGE FILM

- *Father and son coming out of the house with the plane*
- *Medium-distance shot of father holding the plane while the son winds the prop*
- *The son launches the plane and the camera follows it through the air*
- *The plane lands and both father and son run to recover it*
- *Close-up of son checking it over for any possible damage*

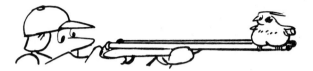

Hunting Trip

- *Close-up of a box of shells on a table*
- *Scene showing a member of the hunting party sitting around home preparing his rifle, checking his telescopic sight, loading the pockets of his jacket with cartridges — close-ups should be interspersed to show details of this activity*

- *Close-up of clock indicating late enough hour for bedtime*
  ADD DAYLIGHT FILTER OR CHANGE FILM
- *The following morning, the party beats its way through the underbrush*
- *Brief scene of someone getting off a shot at a deer*
- *Everyone breaks into a run*
- *Medium-distance shot of the successful hunter checking the antler spread of his deer*
- *Close-up of his pleased face*
- *Members of the party carry the buck off and tie it onto the car*

Christmas Morning

- *Brief scene showing the Christmas tree with gifts around it*
- *The children come racing in and begin opening packages*
- *Close-ups and medium-distance scenes of the children ripping packages open and their responses to the contents*
- *They finally discover a sled and decide they want to try it out*
- *Close-ups and medium-length shots of the children getting into their heavy outer clothing, pulling collars up, and buckling on their high boots*
  ADD DAYLIGHT FILTER OR CHANGE FILM
- *The children come out of the house with their new sled*
- *Medium-distance scene shows the older child pulling the younger*
- *When they try to switch places, the younger has a great deal of difficulty making the sled budge*
- *Mother finally offers to pull both of them and off they go*
- *Final close-up of the happy faces as they go by*

Continued from page 69

. . . with mother's little helper leading the way to the park.

The drinking fountain turned out to be even better than a shower or a swimming pool.

Eventually we wandered over to the children's zoo . . .

. . . but Tommy wasn't completely sure he liked it at first.

He finally discovered, though, that these kids were just like any other kids, and began to warm up a bit.

The burro looked like a pretty friendly old cuss . . .

. . . and once I had given a feeding demonstration, . . .

. . . Tommy was all for going it solo.

We had been feeding animals so much that we finally decided we ought to start feeding boys . . .

. . . and daddies too.

But even the most avid and enthusiastic zoo-goer . . .

. . . eventually poops out.

Chapter VI

Splicing—
making big reels
from
little ones

How to Stop Torturing Family and Friends

Consider your audience. The lights are extinguished and everyone settles back to enjoy your movies. They aren't permitted to
settle very far or very comfortably, though, because four minutes later (only two minutes if you have a 16mm camera using
50 foot loads) on will come the lights again while you rewind
the film and thread a new roll through the projector. This
spasmodic sort of performance is upsetting to the digestion,
not to mention what it will do to one's temper. Even if your
audience is limited to only yourself, it's still something of a
trial.

The necessity of aping a jack-in-the-box every time you project a film can be eliminated by a modest gadget costing little
more than a carton of cigarettes. Called a "splicer," it provides
an easy means of connecting two, three, four, or more brief
reels of home movies into one long, restful reel. Every 8mm
projector is capable of showing at least a 200-foot reel; and
every 16mm projector, at least a 400-foot reel. Both offer more
than 16 minutes of uninterrupted movies.

Splicers featuring varying degrees of convenience at varying
degrees of cost are on display at most camera shops. The
Kodak Junior Splicer, 8mm and 16mm, while certainly neither
de luxe nor frilly, is probably among the least costly and makes
as solid a splice as any. You'll also need a large reel onto which
your spliced small reels can be wound.

Simple splicing can be used for a great deal more than making little reels into big ones. Occasionally, you may find that a roll of processed movies will have short sections of completely black or color-streaked film at the beginning or end. On 8mm reels, these sections may also occur in the middle of the 50 feet, where the two 25-foot strips have been joined. This is generally caused by incorrect loading procedures, either running off too much of the protective outer layers of film before you begin shooting or permitting light to reach your film. With a splicer, you can quickly cut such areas out of your movies.

It's extremely important that all film be placed in the splicer *dull* side up. Film splices are actually welds, and splicing cement isn't a real adhesive but rather a solvent that dissolves the base of both strips of film so that, when you press them together, they form an extremely strong connection. When film is dull side up, you are looking at the thin light-sensitive material (called emulsion) which is attached to the transparent base and creates the picture. After you scrape this emulsion off the left-hand strip of film, apply cement, and press the back of the right-hand strip on top of it, base is meeting base and a satisfactory weld results.

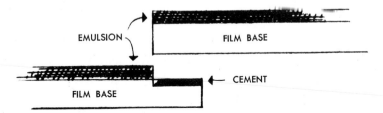

EMULSION

FILM BASE

FILM BASE

CEMENT

After the thin coating of light-sensitive emulsion has been scraped off an area, cement can be applied which will weld base to base.

A pair of rewinds, or even one, will be a great convenience for splicing work. These are devices that hold the reels of film while you are splicing so that you can quickly wind the spliced film onto its large reel. A good pair of rewinds will cost about ten dollars.

75

To make a handy splicing outfit, obtain a board about two to three feet long and anchor your splicer in the center. Then merely screw one rewind to each end, paint the board white and you're set. If you don't feel like investing in the rewinds, you might fasten vertical pieces of wood about six inches high to each side of the board and drive a fairly long nail through these pieces near the top. The nails could serve as axes for two reels which could be spun by your finger.

These same splicing techniques can be employed for inserting titles, trimming out undesirable or uninteresting footage, rearranging scenes, and performing dozens of other tasks, all of which come under the classification of "Editing and Titling." There's a special chapter on this that begins on page 126.

Making a Splice

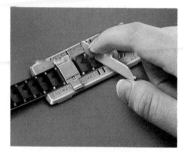 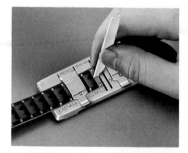

Raise the Junior Splicer's two clamps and, from the left, feed the start of one reel into the splicer, dull side up. All of the white, celluloid-type material should be to the right of the splicer's left-hand slot. Slip the film perforations over the five pins farthest left and lower the left clamp. Insert the cutting end of the cutting tool into the left-hand slot and cut.

Moisten a narrow strip at the edge of the film from which you have just removed the white, celluloid-type material. Scrape this strip by slipping the scraper end of the cutting tool into the left-hand slot and pushing it back and forth. Continue scraping until all of the blue-green coating (actually the film's emulsion) has been removed and the strip is clear.

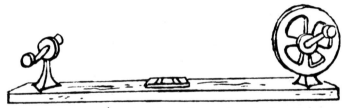

A splicing outfit made with a splicer and a pair of rewinds.

A splicing outfit using nails as axes on which the reels can turn.

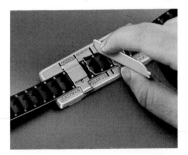

Then raise the right clamp and insert the tail end of the other reel, the reel you want projected first, into the splicer dull side up so that it just overlaps the start of the other film. The perforations should slip over the three pins farthest right. Lower the right clamp and cut the film by operating the cutting end of the cutting tool in the right-hand slot.

Lift the right clamp and move the right film so that its end overlaps the scraped portion of the left film. Its perforations should again fit over the three right-hand pins. Lower the right clamp and raise the end of the right film slightly. Apply a little cement on the scraped end of the left film, press the right film down, and hold them in contact for 20 seconds.

Chapter VII

Showing Your Movies

The Basic Facts of Projection

A recently published cartoon depicted a harried moviemaker up to his kneecaps in loose film, pouring manually over the remainder of his collection while his wife confided to a visitor, "I guess we'll just have to break down and buy Henry a projector." In case you've ever been in this predicament, be assured that there's nothing quite like projection for getting a good look at your movies.

During the past few years our viewing horizons have been stretched almost beyond recognition by the television and motion picture industries, which have produced in most people a definite taste for big pictures. Although home movie projectors can deliver enough sheer size to satisfy almost anyone, they do have definite limits. One of the most basic is that 8mm movies cannot be projected satisfactorily to a width greater than about five feet.

This, of course, is no great handicap when you are thinking entirely in terms of a home audience, but it explains why 16mm equipment is recommended to anyone contemplating screenings to large groups in large halls. Not only is each 16mm movie frame four times the area of an 8mm frame, but more powerful projectors are manufactured for 16mm film than 8mm. The combination of these factors makes it possible to project 16mm

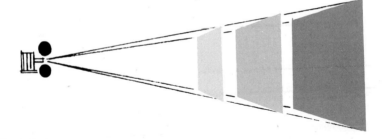

As a movie projector is moved farther from a screen, its picture will become progressively larger but also less brilliant.

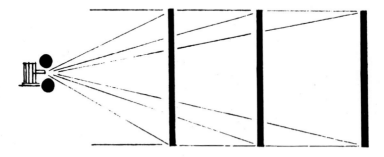

The shorter the focal length of a projection lens, the shorter the distance required for it to fill a screen with the picture.

movies to widths of 20 feet. Three elements which govern image dimension are:

- ILLUMINATION PRODUCED BY PROJECTOR — *the greater the amount of light produced by a projector, the farther it will "throw" an acceptable image.*
- PROJECTOR-TO-SCREEN DISTANCE — *the farther from the projector to the screen, the larger the picture.*
- FOCAL LENGTH OF THE PROJECTOR LENS — *the shorter the focal length, the larger the picture at equal projector-to-screen distances; although the conventional focal lengths are one inch for 8mm projectors and two inches for 16mm, all of the current Brownie Movie Projectors have three-quarter inch lenses, often a desirable feature when showing films in rather small rooms.*

PROJECTION DISTANCES AND PICTURE WIDTH

Projector-to-screen distance in feet	8mm projector 3/4" lens 16mm projector 1½" lens	8mm projector 1" lens 16mm projector 2" lens	16mm projector 3" lens
8	2'0"	1'6"	
10	2'6"	1'10"	1'3"
12	3'0"	2'3"	1'6"
16	4'0"	3'0"	2'0"
20	5'0"	3'9"	2'6"
25		4'8"	3'1"

As might be guessed, the brighter the lamp used in a projector, the brighter also will be the picture it projects. Before you adopt the assumption that the most powerful lamp is automatically the most desirable, consider that the heat output, as well as the light output, of a 1,000-watt lamp is twice that of a 500-watt. Each projector is made for use with lamps of only a certain maximum wattage. If higher wattage lamps should be installed, the greater heat levels they create are likely to be beyond the capacities of the blower systems and heat-absorbing glass; therefore, they may endanger both the film and the projector.

Screens and Screenings

Not many rooms are large enough to permit the projection of home movies to a width much greater than three feet except with such equipment as the Brownie Movie Projectors. One easy means of increasing the size of the screen image in any room is to place projector and screen in opposite corners and project diagonally. In a 12 by 16-foot room, for example, the diagonal dimension would be four feet greater than the longest wall. Another expedient for achieving a large picture is to place the projector in a room adjoining the one in which your screen is situated and project through the doorway.

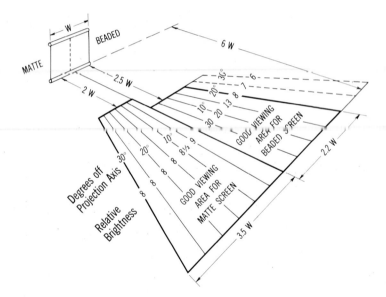

For best visibility of a movie projected onto a beaded screen, members of the audience should be seated close to the projector-screen axis. With a matte screen the picture will not be as brilliant, but members of the audience may sit in a more spread-out pattern.

The appearance of a movie has a good deal to do with the surface on which it is projected. Beaded and aluminized screens provide a more sparkling, brilliant color image than matte screens, but they require that the viewers all be seated quite close to the line between the projector and screen.

Few makeshift screens provide nearly as good a picture as the real article, but white artist's mounting board and walls painted with flat white paint are fairly satisfactory substitutes. Colored walls inevitably degrade and tint the colors in the movie. Bed sheets, table cloths, or window shades may be used in an emergency, but, because much of the light from the projector passes through them, they cannot give you the same sort of picture as is obtained on an opaque surface.

Threading and operating procedure varies considerably from projector to projector, but the instruction booklets packaged with most of them contain clear, well illustrated instructions that should be followed closely. One recommendation applicable to all projection equipment is that, at the end of a movie, the lamp should be turned off but the motor kept operating for a few minutes. This permits the cooling fan to reduce the temperature of both the internal and external parts.

Three Suggestions For Good Shows

- Set up, thread, and focus your projector before your audience comes into the room, so that you're ready to start as soon as they're seated.
- When a reel ends and you plan to show another, don't rewind the first, but immediately thread the second. Both can be rewound later.
- Don't subject friends or acquaintances to overly long family films or movies of very restricted interest.

Part II

Chapter VIII

The mechanics of making good movies

Loading Your Camera

If you have an 8mm roll-film camera, the box of Kodachrome Film that provides you with 50 feet of 8mm movies actually contains 33 feet of specially perforated 16mm film. Before your mind begins to wander to visions of film shrinkers and picture stretchers, be assured that there's a more logical explanation.

The original width of the film is 16mm because it is designed to run through the camera twice, producing two side-by-side strips of movies. After processing these are slit apart and spliced into a continuous strip.

An application of simple arithmetic would make it seem, then, that a roll of 8mm film would yield 66 feet of color movies. Actually, though, there is an extra 4 feet of film 16mm wide provided at each end of the roll to do nothing more than protect the inner 25 feet from being light-struck during loading and unloading. At the processing laboratory, this extra footage is removed after your film leaves the processing machine.

On a roll of 8mm film, the outermost (A) and innermost (C) 4 feet protect the inner 25 feet (B) from being light-struck.

After a roll of 8mm film has run through your camera once, all of it will be on a spool marked with a reminder that only half of the film has been exposed. This full spool should be removed from the camera, turned over, and reloaded just as if it were a new roll of film. Turning it over is essential, since this insures that each side of the film will be exposed once, rather than one side twice, but, even if you should forget this step, you'll find it quite difficult to slip the spool on incorrectly due to the design of the spool itself and the upper spindle.

Standard 16mm roll film travels through the camera only once, but it also has an extra length of film at each end for protective purposes. Do not ever attempt to load regular 16mm film in an 8mm camera. It does not have the same perforations as the film packaged specifically for 8mm cameras and will not move through the camera.

Before being slit, 8mm film contains two rows of side-by-side movies. It is the same width as 16mm film but has different perforations.

16mm   8mm UNSLIT

There are only a few important checkpoints in loading a magazine-type camera. With 8mm cameras, be sure that the two openings at the front of the magazine are closed. Should any film be visible, rotate the metal pin between them until they are completely covered. Always be certain that you start an 8mm magazine with the number 1 side face up and never remove the tape that encircles the magazine.

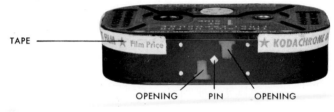

TAPE

OPENING   PIN   OPENING

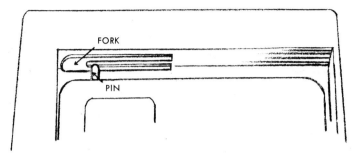

FORK

PIN

With 16mm cameras, see that the pin atop the magazine slips into the fork inside the camera. If it doesn't, the camera will jam.

Loading a roll film camera quickly and efficiently takes a bit of dexterity. Here's one good method.

With a finger pressed over the side of the film on the new spool, orient it so that it turns *clockwise* when you draw off about a foot or a foot-and-a-half of film. Slip the end of this film into the notch of the empty spool (for an 8mm camera make sure that the side of the empty spool facing up is the one that reads "Film when on this spool is only half exposed") and, turning the empty spool also *clockwise,* take two turns of film around the core. Then, with one finger still making certain that the film does not unwind, drop the full spool over the camera's upper spindle, slide the film into the film gate (see below), drop the empty spool over the lower spindle, and rotate it *clockwise* to take up the slack film. Run a few inches of film to be certain everything is as it should be, close the camera, and use the system explained in your instruction booklet for running off the remaining outer protective film before you begin shooting.

In a roll-film camera, the film must be slipped in front of the pressure pad. The spring behind this pad then holds the film flat against the aperture plate. This channel into which the film goes is called the "film gate."

87

Films

If, in the strange meanderings of conversation, any of us ever speaks of light, we generally treat it as being all of one kind, plain old white light. Actually, though, there is an amazing variety of color among the light sources we cram into the 'plain old white light' category — a tribute, of sorts, to the eye and its ability to ignore subtle phenomena if they are encountered frequently enough.

The romantic flicker of a candle is much warmer (yellow-red) in color than the light from the 100-watt bulb in your kitchen which, in turn, is yellower than the illumination produced by the PH-375 photoflood lamps you probably use, or should use, for indoor moviemaking. Even sunlight, though not subject to the whims of manufacturers and consumers, isn't entirely uniform in color under different atmospheric conditions. Although nearly all forms are cooler (bluer) than the light from photoflood or tungsten lamps, a hazy or cloudy sky will cause cooler illumination than clear conditions, and, in the opposite direction, a sunset or sunrise may, at times, create light that is warmer in tone than that of a candle.

For a color film to reproduce a subject's colors as naturally as it is capable of doing, it must be balanced for the kind of light illuminating that subject. This principle might mean that we would need dozens of types of a color film such as Kodachrome, one for each different kind of light bulb or a different type of daylight. Actually, we are able to sidestep this form of photographic redundance and limit the number of types of Kodachrome Film to two.

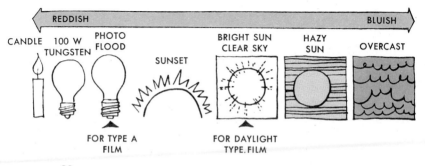

First, we standardize our light sources. Photoflood lamps, because of their size, brightness, and the fact that they are made in so many useful types, are just about ideal for home movie shooting, so Kodachrome Film, Type A, is compounded to do its best under this kind of illumination. Kodachrome Film, Daylight Type, has been balanced primarily for bright sunlight with a clear sky overhead, but the difference between the color of this light and the illumination on hazy or cloudy days is generally so slight that the difference isn't greatly noticeable. During the two or three hours of sunrise or sunset, however, the light is likely to be much warmer in tone and, unless you are shooting scenics, special effects shots, or really want the increased redness in your movies, it's advisable to save your film.

The other subterfuge involves the use of filters. If, for example, you were shooting some outdoor movies in bright sunlight, but suddenly found that your subjects had moved into an area of bluish shade, you could make the cool shaded colors look normal to the film by simply placing a pale pink filter, such as the Kodak Skylight Filter (No. 1A), over the camera's lens.

As mentioned previously, the most popular and useful application of filters in color moviemaking is the Kodak Daylight Filter for Kodak Type A Color Films (No. 85), a salmon-colored "monocle," which permits you to expose Type A film by sunlight and makes it possible to do all of your shooting on one type of Kodachrome Film.

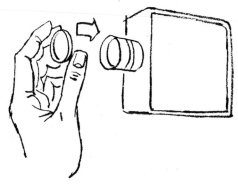

In deep shade, use a Kodak Skylight Filter (No. 1A) over the camera lens to reduce bluishness. When you have Type A film in your camera and wish to shoot pictures outdoors, slip a Kodak Daylight Filter for Kodak Type A Color Films (No. 85) over the lens.

Exposure

The start of a picture occurs when light reflects off a subject, travels through the camera lens, and strikes the film. For colors to turn out bright and natural-looking, the same amount of light must reach the film every time you press the button.

Unhappily, though, light varies tremendously under different conditions. On a sunny day there may be sixteen times as much of it as on an overcast day. Indoors, when shooting with a light bar, you reduce the illumination on your subject by three-quarters when you shift from a three-foot to a six-foot range.

Nothing practical can be done to hold the light level steady, so the best alternative is one of regulating the size of the opening through which light enters the camera lens. The principle is something like this: if you want a certain amount of illumination in your living room, you pull the shade nearly all the way down on a sunny day, but roll it all the way up when the weather is cloudy.

A variety of lens openings can be provided either by attaching a wheel over the camera lens that, when turned, places holes of different size in front of the lens (as on the Brownie Movie Cameras) or by building inside the lens an iris diaphragm that opens and closes. The settings that mark these openings are identified by a numbering system which relates the effective

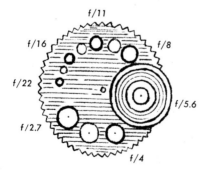

Lens openings on Brownie Movie Cameras are changed by rotating a wheel that has holes of varying size.

The lens opening on many cameras is adjusted by the use of a multi-blade iris diaphragm inside the lens.

diameter of the opening with the focal length* of the lens. For example, if a lens has a focal length of 25 mm and the lens opening is 3 mm in diameter, it will be marked $f/8$, or 8. The arithmetical workings go like this:

$3/25 = f/8$, or just plain 8

When the opening is larger, say 12 mm, the marking would be:

$12/25 = f/2$, or 2

The larger the lens opening, then, the smaller the f-number that designates it. In the following series, probably similar to the one on your camera, each succeeding smaller number represents twice as wide an opening as the previous number: 22, 16, 11, 8, 5.6, 4, 2.8, 2, 1.4. One of the beauties of this system is that it makes the same exposure recommendations applicable to all cameras and to lenses of all focal length.

A different lens setting will be needed for each of the main types of daylight. The definitions of these types are included in the chart below. Appropriate lens settings are also shown beneath the chart. For indoor shooting, the lens opening will depend upon how many lamps your light bar accommodates and on the distance from the lights to your subject. The exposure table for indoor shooting is given on the next page. All of this data is condensed in the *Kodak Movie Dial* and the wider-ranging *Kodak Movie Photoguide*, both pocket-sized and both sold in most camera shops.

Focal length is the distance from a certain point in the lens to the film when the lens is focused on a distant point.

Bright Sun 8	**Hazy Sun** 5.6	**Cloudy Bright** 4	**Open Shade** 2.8
The sun is bright; all shadows are dark. For sand and snow conditions, see page 27.	The sun's disk is visible but softened by thin clouds. Shadows are light.	The sun is obscured by clouds. There are no shadows. Still, there's fairly bright light.	The subject is in a shaded area but has clear, brightly lighted sky directly overhead.

INDOOR LENS SETTINGS Kodachrome Movie Film, Type A

Distance in Feet	3	4	6	9	13
2 Lamps	8	5.6	4	2.7 or 2.8	1.9 or 2
4 Lamps	11	8	5.6	4	2.7 or 2.8

Lamps should be 375-watt Medium-Beam, Reflector-Type Photofloods

You may wonder whether an exposure meter is necessary for good movies. As long as you do all of your outdoor shooting by sunlight and your indoor shooting with a photo light bar, a meter would merely confirm the data in the exposure tables. But, if you frequently make movies in the shade, in overcast weather, or indoors by photofloods in stands, a meter is essential for consistently good results, since it provides a reliable means of measuring the amount of light present and converting that measurement into terms of a lens opening.

Many different kinds of meters are available, from simple types planned for use with only a limited number of films (Kodachrome is almost always one of them) to more complex instruments, extremely sensitive and adaptable to a wide range of movie and snapshot situations. All meters, however, have certain common characteristics — a photoelectric cell which measures the intensity of the light and a need of being set for both the kind of film in your camera and the camera speed.

Various kinds of film have different degrees of sensitivity to light. This sensitivity is expressed by a number, called an "exposure index," always printed on the film instruction sheet. This index must be set on an exposure meter.

EXPOSURE INDEXES Kodachrome Movie Films

	Daylight	Tungsten
Kodachrome Film, Daylight Type	10	5*
Kodachrome Film, Type A	10†	16

*With Kodak Photoflood Filter for Kodak Daylight Type Color Films (No. 80B).
†With Kodak Daylight Filter for Kodak Type A Color Films (No. 85).

The normal camera speed for home movie shooting is 16 frames per second. Many meters are specially marked not only for this but for the other frequently used movie speeds as well. When no such mark appears on a meter, it should be set about halfway between still camera shutter times of 1/25 and 1/50.

Before using a meter, absorb the content of its instruction booklet thoroughly. Unless properly employed, a meter will be no more helpful than an outright guess and might be worse.

The simplest means of making an outdoor reading is to aim the cell of the meter toward the bottom of the subject and move it slowly upward. At a certain point, the meter needle will move rapidly toward the high end of the scale. Use the reading you get just before the needle does this. This jump occurs when the cell begins to "see" the comparatively bright sky and, unless the reading caused by the sky is ignored in obtaining the lens setting, the other parts of the subject will be greatly underexposed.

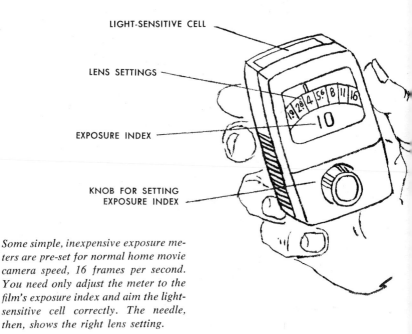

LIGHT-SENSITIVE CELL

LENS SETTINGS

EXPOSURE INDEX

KNOB FOR SETTING
EXPOSURE INDEX

Some simple, inexpensive exposure meters are pre-set for normal home movie camera speed, 16 frames per second. You need only adjust the meter to the film's exposure index and aim the light-sensitive cell correctly. The needle, then, shows the right lens setting.

A reflected light reading is made by pointing the meter cell toward the subject. Care must be taken to avoid having the bright sky influence outdoor readings.

An incident light reading is made by holding the meter so that its cell points halfway between the camera position and the main source of illumination.

The system described above, called the "reflected light method" since it measures light reflecting from the subject, is fine outdoors, but, when an indoor subject is lighted by photofloods, a reflected light reading may be overly influenced by a dark, relatively unilluminated background and lead to overexposure. In such situations and also when there is very little light present, it's desirable to measure the light on its way toward the subject. This is called the "incident light method." Many, but not all, meters are designed to make both kinds of readings. If your meter can be used for incident-light readings, hold it in the same location as the subject and point the cell halfway between the camera and the main source of light.

If your meter isn't designed for incident light readings, point the palm of your hand about halfway between the camera and the main source of light and make a reflected-light reading from a distance of about 4 to 6 inches. If your movie scene is going to be chiefly a close-up of someone's face, use the reading you get without change. If not, use one setting *more* exposure than the reading indicates (e.g., 2.8 if the reading calls for 4).

The published exposure indexes are not sacred cows. If you find that your movies, roll after roll, are consistently a bit dark, try a lower index, say 8 rather than 10 for Kodachrome Film used outdoors; if they are consistently light, try a higher one, perhaps 12.

Critical Exposure Adjustments

| Front Lighting | Side Lighting | Back Lighting |

Under front lighting, the subject faces the sun. Under side lighting the sun is at the side and under back lighting it is behind the subject. Most movie makers are satisfied to use the setting given in exposure tables (actually the setting for front lighting) with all three. If critical accuracy is desired, though, the lens opening should be a half-setting wider for side lighting, a full setting wider for back lighting.

| Light Subject | Average Subject | Dark Subject |

A light subject consists primarily of light-colored areas, a dark subject of dark-colored or shadowed areas. Most movie makers treat all subjects as average (nearly all are) and use the same lens setting for all subjects that are under the same kind of lighting. If critical accuracy is desired, though, the lens opening should be a half-setting smaller for a light subject, a half-setting wider for a dark subject.

95

Viewfinding

The only feature even faintly tricky about your camera view-finder is that you simply don't see exactly the same picture through it that the film sees through the lens. The reason? Simply because the finder is generally located about two inches above the lens. While this situation, called "parallax," may seem to present all sorts of intriguing and irritating problems, be assured that it actually causes few. It really has no practical effect on all but a very small proportion of most people's movie-making.

The view through the finder varies from the view through the lens by inches. Only in extreme close-ups will these inches be critical.

The difference between what you see and what the lens sees is only about two inches on most cameras. No matter whether your subject is twenty-four feet away or twenty-four inches away, there will always be two inches at the top (as you view it through your finder) that, in the final movie, will be replaced by two inches' worth that is just beneath the bottom of your view. But, at twenty-four feet, those two inches are only two inches of a subject area about seven feet high and can be ignored; at twenty-four inches, though, they account for about a third of a picture area only about six inches in height, and, unless you do something corrective, you may inadvertently be cutting off and losing some important part of your intended picture.

Quite a few cameras have built-in aids to help overcome this problem. One of them is a little mark on the side and near the top of the viewfinder. For extreme close-ups, usually at three feet or less, you should line up the top of your picture with this mark rather than the actual frame of the finder. Another type of aid is an adjustable rear sight which can be raised or lowered for different camera-to-subject distances. Ordinarily, there will be five or six varied settings on this kind of rear finder, but for

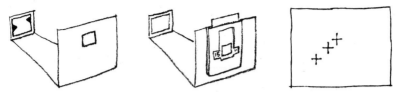

Parallax compensating viewfinder devices may be pips against which to line up the top of the picture at close range; movable rear sights which can be raised for close-up shooting; reticles containing off-center marks on which to center close-up scenes.

all of your ordinary shooting you can keep it at the position marked for 15 feet and change it only when the shooting distance becomes three feet or less, the point at which this parallax effect becomes significant enough to make a difference.

If your camera does not have some sort of aid for really close close-up shooting, the best thing to do about parallax is simply forget it until you wish to shoot something at three feet or less. Then merely aim the camera a little higher than the top of the subject and your film will probably turn out quite nicely.

Winding the Spring Motor

It's a noble rule (already stated and restated on page 13) to crank the spring motor of your camera after every scene so that it will be fully wound. This insures that you'll never be frustrated by a "pooped-out" camera in the midst of some scintillating snapping.

Like nearly all noble rules, though, this one is far from immune to the press of circumstance. You might be shooting some critical few moments in a Little League ball game. Scenes may come so close together that they don't permit time for winding or else you may often find that, after running the camera for a while, you're often waiting eye-to-viewfinder for some special action to occur, with the chance that you might miss it if you lowered the camera to wind it. If you do have an opportunity to wind, it may not be long enough for a full winding.

In unusual situations like this, it's handy to know how much shooting time you'll be able to get from the few windings you are able to make. Most movie cameras run between 7 and 12 feet of film on a full winding — the instruction booklet usually provides the exact information. At a camera speed of 16 frames per second, each foot of 8mm film takes 5 seconds, each foot of 16mm film, 2½ seconds. If you count the number of winding turns needed to bring your camera from a wound-down to a fully wound condition and divide the total into the number of seconds of movies obtained from a full winding, you'll know how much each winding provides.

For example, a Brownie Movie Camera handles 10 feet of film on a full winding. This is 48 seconds' worth. About 35 half-turns of the winding handle fully wind the spring, and when 48 is divided by 35 the significance of the quotient, approximately 1½, is that each half-turn furnishes about 1½ seconds of camera operation. Therefore, if you've had time for eight half-turns, you can count on being able to shoot at least 12 seconds of movies before the camera runs down.

The importance of this isn't actually in knowing the precise number of seconds of moviemaking obtained from a certain amount of wrist-twisting. Its usefulness comes from indicating that, while one or two turns won't be enough for an average-length scene, six, or eight, or some other number will.

Camera Handling

Human hands have proven capable of clamping around such diverse objects as submarine sandwiches, bowling balls, and greased pigs. They certainly, then, should have no difficulty in providing the firm fondling required by a home movie camera, in spite of its possible peculiarities of size and shape. A steady camera is an essential prerequisite of steady movies, and there's a certain arrangement of hands, wrists, and arms that fits each and every one. Chances are that your camera instruction booklet illustrates a comfortable and efficient way of holding your own particular piece of moviemaking machinery, but here are a few principles that apply almost universally.

One hand should support the camera from beneath to prevent it from jiggling up and down. In most instances, the picture button is located so that it can be operated easily by a finger of this hand. The lower arm should be vertical, and the upper arm braced close against the chest for extra support from the body.

The other hand should wrap itself around the back and one side of the camera to guard against swaying. This lower arm should also be vertical, with the upper arm tight against the side of the body. It's extremely important to do your movie snapping with arms held in close.

Don't ever swing your camera around in the casual way you might handle a garden hose. The *only* time to move the camera rapidly is when you are following some fast-moving subject. If you try it on subjects that are relatively fixed, the effect will be about the same as attempting to get a good look at a railroad station from the window of a train that's racing past at 60 miles per hour. When you want to show all of some large subject in your movie, step farther back so that it will fit into your viewfinder. If this isn't possible, aim your camera at one side and then move it toward the other at an extremely slow rate. You'll notice that the professional cameramen who produce the films on display in movie theaters and for television always handle the problem in this way.

Also, never walk while you're shooting unless you're willing to accept a jarringly bumpy movie. You can, however, make some wonderfully effective films from moving cars and trains if you aim primarily at distant subjects. Results are generally best if you shoot through an open window (preferably at 24 frames per second), but, when this isn't possible, simply make sure that the window you choose has no noticeable reflections on it, since these will appear in your movies, and, if possible, that it isn't tinted.

Focusing

A lens is more than a mere window. The characteristic that distinguishes it from other slices of glassware is that it possesses the ability to focus. At some certain distance behind a lens, it will project a sharp, distinct picture of some of the things that are in front of it, and the location at which it projects this picture is the one where we want the film to be.

But, when a lens projects a picture, only objects one certain distance from that lens will be absolutely sharp. Everything in front of and behind the plane on which those objects fall will be progressively less and less sharp. The distance to this

99

At a small lens opening such as 8 or 5.6, the range of sharpness will be extensive; at a large opening such as 2 it will be narrow.

plane is called the "focus," and any lens is basically capable of being focused at almost any distance.

Fortunately, in most instances, many of the objects in front of and behind the focus distance will be so nearly as sharp as those right at the focus distance that, in looking at a picture, you simply cannot tell the difference. This provides, for practical purposes, a range of sharpness.

The extent of this range of sharpness depends on two factors: the actual distance for which the lens is focused and the size of the lens opening. If the lens is focused for some close-up distance, the range is rather shallow; when it is focused for a farther distance, the range becomes much greater. In addition, if the lens opening is a small one of the kind you'd use outdoors on a sunny day—say, $f/8$, or 8—the range will be greater than if the lens was focused at the exact same distance but the opening required was larger—say, $f/2.8$, or 2.8.

The existence of this range makes possible fixed-focus movie cameras, such as those in the Brownie Movie series. On these cameras, the lens focusing is preset at the factory on some intermediate distance which provides as great a range of sharpness as possible through all of the various lens openings. The far limit of sharpness at all lens openings is as far away as your eye can see (infinity); the near limits vary, depending upon the opening, and are shown in the chart on the next page.

100

NEAREST SHOOTING DISTANCES with Fixed-Focus 8mm Movie Cameras

Lens Settings	1.9 or 2	2.3	2.7 or 2.8	4	5.6	8	11	16
Distance in Feet	**10**	**8½**	**8**	**6**	**4½**	**3½**	**2½**	**2**

On most cameras with lenses that require focusing, it is generally easy to see just what your range of sharpness will be. Before shooting any scene, you will, of course, either check the sunlight or estimate the distance from your light bar to the subject and obtain the correct lens opening. Next, you judge the distance to the subject and set that distance opposite the little index mark on the focusing scale. Now, look at the scale immediately alongside the one with the focusing distances. It consists of lens opening numbers going in both directions from the index mark, starting with the widest openings and ending with the narrowest. If you check the distances on the focusing scale opposite the actual lens opening you are using, they will tell you the limits of your range of sharpness.

This scale is most helpful in cases where there are important parts of a picture subject at different distances from the camera. It may turn out that, at the particular focus distance you have set, only one will be sharp, but that, by adjusting the focus slightly, you will be able to bring both distances into the range of sharpness.

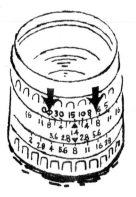

On many focusing lenses there are lens setting numbers going in both directions from the focus index mark. The footage distances on the focusing scale opposite the actual lens setting being used mark off the range of focus. Here, at a setting of 8, it would be from 6 to infinity.

101

Camera Speeds

When a home movie is made at the rate of 16 frames (individual pictures) per second and then projected at this same rate, all action tends to look smooth and to duplicate the pace at which it actually occurred. If a movie is made at 32 frames per second, though, and projected at 16, all of the action appears to be taking place at a much slower rate, chiefly because it has been split up into a greater number of individual pictures. This is what makes slow motion look slow.

A camera set for slow motion shooting at, say, 32 frames per second, simply runs the film through at a speed twice normal. Should you expose an entire roll of 8mm film at 32 frames, it will be consumed in two minutes rather than the customary four. You will, however, get four minutes of movies on your projection screen as long as the projector is operated at the standard 16 frames per second.

There's another important effect of slow motion shooting. Each individual frame is exposed to light for a shorter period. At 32 frames it will be in front of the lens for only half as long as at 16. Unless some sort of compensating adjustment is made, a scene shot at 32 frames will turn out extremely dark due to

The more rapid the action, the more fascinating that a slow-motion perusal of it will be. Slow-motion movies are an ideal means of checking your sports form. For most action, 32 frames per second will be sufficient. To check a golf swing, though, try 48 or 64.

underexposure. We can compensate for this by opening the lens to the next *larger* setting than it would be for 16 frames so that, although each frame will be exposed for only half as long, it will receive just as much light during exposure. Thus far, all of the recommended lens settings in this book have been based on shooting at 16 frames per second. Those in the table below are applicable to the other most frequently used camera speeds.

LENS SETTINGS FOR SLOW-MOTION CAMERA SPEEDS

When recommended setting at 16 Frames is:	USE SETTINGS BELOW AT			
	64 Frames	48 Frames	32 Frames	24 Frames
11	5.6	5.6–8	8	8–11
8	4	4–5.6	5.6	5.6–8
5.6	2.7 or 2.8	2.7–4 or 2.8–4	4	4–5.6
4	1.9 or 2	2–2.7 or 2–2.8	2.7 or 2.8	2.7–4 or 2.8–4
2.7 or 2.8	1.4	1.4–1.9 or 1.4–2	1.9 or 2	2–2.7 or 2–2.8

Each hyphenated setting is halfway between numbers shown.

If your camera does offer a variety of speeds, try slow motion first on sports subjects. You'll probably find that 32 frames per second will do nicely for a swimmer, diver, skier, and, in fact, any but the most rapid action. When shooting something extremely fast moving like a golfer's or ball player's swing, shift over to 48 or 64 frames. A good way to introduce a slow motion sequence, if the action can be performed twice in a row, is to shoot it first at normal speed and then repeat it in slow motion.

Use of camera speeds slower than 16 frames per second is pretty much limited to comedy effects. Any motion photographed at 12 or 8 frames will be speeded up and will appear quite choppy, in the style of the Keystone Cops.

Chapter IX

Making movies more interesting

The Camera Tells the Story

In most cinema palaces, the popcorn vendor probably excites more conversation than the cameraman who photographed the movie. The patrons of movie theatres have come to expect that the camera will be in the right place at the right time to help the actors, directors, and writers get on with the story.

Of course, a professional cameraman does have some great advantages, not the least being that whenever anything goes other than the way it should, he has a second chance. So if Slimy McSweeney, the menace, happens accidentally to clobber the Abilene Kid in the climactic fisticuffs, they can be shot all over again.

But this involves other people's mistakes and doesn't bear on home moviemaking in which you generally take activity the way it comes. The important fact about the professional is that he tries to photograph each bit of the action in a way that will help advance the story and help the audience appreciate the comedy or drama of that story, such as it is.

In home movies, though, too often the interesting things that go on in front of the lens are obscured or lessened in impact simply because the camera is handled in a casual, almost careless way. There are three basic means by which to avoid this: variation of scene length, shifts in subject distance, and continuity.

None of these involve rigid, immutable rules. All come pretty naturally, and the more that you use them and see the results on your screen, the better moviemaker you'll become. When you begin trying them out, you'll find, perhaps to your surprise, that it really is just about as easy to shoot a good home movie as a so-so one.

Subject Distance

Before storming into a full-scale discussion of camera-to-subject distances, it probably would be advisable to make a token bow to clarity and re-define the three bits of photographic jargon most constantly exercised in explorations of this subject.

CLOSE-UP—In movies, this is a shot made about 6 feet or less from the subject. At 6 feet, with a lens of normal focal length (12 mm or 13 mm for 8mm shooting, 25 mm for 16mm cameras), most cameras will take in head and shoulders of an adult.

MEDIUM-DISTANCE SHOT—Anything snapped from 25 feet or less but not as close as 6 feet, is a "medium shot." At 25 feet, your camera covers a top-to-bottom dimension of about 6 feet.

LONG-DISTANCE SHOT—A scene of any subject farther away than 25 feet is a long shot.

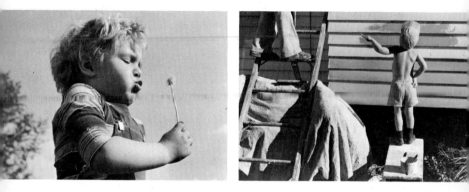

All of these are scaled to the photographing of people. A close-up of the Statue of Liberty might be made from much farther away than 6 feet. The definitions are designed to fit like a stretch sock rather than a kid glove. Particularly under "medium-distance shot" is there a vast amount of latitude, and the category probably could be subdivided into "close-medium," "medium-medium," and "long-medium," but, if this were done, the chapter would begin to look more like an exercise in handling a yardstick than a collection of helpful hints on the relatively free-style pastime of making home movies.

One of the simplest things you can do that will effect the greatest improvement in your movies is to stock them amply with close-ups. At least one scene in every three or four should be a close-up. With a movie camera, close-up shooting is especially easy because, for a head-and-shoulders shot, you can be as far as 6 feet away, a distance from which you aren't too likely to give your subject twinges of self-consciousness. For the same kind of shot with a still camera, you'd have to be nearer than 3 feet.

A good formula, very often, is to start some movie sequence with a long shot to establish location, follow with a medium shot to show what's going on, and then move in for a close-up or two to pinpoint action. This can't be applied to every situation, but it does fit a great many.

CLOSE-UP: *This is usually made from 6 feet or nearer, includes head and shoulders of a person.* MEDIUM-DISTANCE SHOT: *This can be made at a distance of from 6 to 25 feet, can show an adult in standing position.* LONG-DISTANCE SHOT: *This is made at a shooting distance of more than 25 feet.*

Actually, the best distance from which to shoot a scene is the closest distance that provides a complete view of whatever is occurring. When shooting a certain activity, this distance will frequently change, and so should your camera position.

This sounds like nothing but common sense. But, the more movies you make, the more evident it will become that the best are those in which you apply such rules of common sense by varying camera-to-subject distance, spicing your shooting with close-ups, and shooting each slice of activity from the nearest distance which permits you to include all important elements.

Continuity

"Continuity" uses five syllables to express what "story" does in two. Whenever a series of scenes has some sort of basic unity, usually because it shows the progress of a certain activity, and if the scenes appear in logical sequence, you have a natural story and natural continuity.

The alternative is a collection of moving snapshots with nothing linking them but the film itself. Once the owner of a movie camera finds that the original novelty of just being able to make pictures that *move* has begun to pall, such snapshot reels are likely to start seeming rather dull and boring.

If, when your mind juggles together the words "movie" and "continuity," visions appear of elaborate scenarios, Cecil B. DeMille in puttees, and a cast of thousands, sit down, relax, and regroup your thoughts. For the kind of home movie continuity in which most people are interested, no rehearsals and no heavy planning are needed. Occasionally, though, a social director's knack of keeping things moving comes in handy.

In many instances, all the action needed for a good film will be entirely impromptu. In others, it may be necessary to have some scenes acted out specially, either because they add something that makes the movie more interesting or to repeat a happening that occurred, perhaps, when you were too far away or not in a position to shoot. Often, too, continuity can be enhanced by removing certain sections of film entirely or even by rearranging the order of some scenes. The why's and how's of this are covered in the chapter on editing which begins on page 126.

Although the lily can sometimes be gilded by having certain scenes acted out or by editing, the foundation of a good home movie is still natural activity. If you're intent on making your films as interesting as possible, you've got to start with more than a mere decision to shoot some movies, period. Either you must wait for some interesting activity to start spontaneously or take a hand in starting it yourself.

There are several common tricks you can use to help promote a feeling of smooth continuity in your movies. For example, whenever the setting is going to change from indoors to outdoors or vice versa, end one scene with the subject going through a door and then, when you begin the next one in the new setting, it will tend to make much more sense. If the setting is going to change between two scenes but will remain indoors or outdoors, merely let the subject walk right out of the picture area in one setting and, when you start the next scene, have the subject walk into the picture area, preferably from a different angle, although the same direction. You may find the "Movie Organizer" in the *Kodak Movie Photoguide* to be helpful as you start striving for greater story unity.

Basically, though, nearly all of the continuity you will ever need is built right into the activities that lend themselves to good home movies. It's just a matter of confining your moviemaking to these activities and occasionally adding to the normal proceedings a few ideas that will make the story more interesting.

Scene Length

While it's easy enough to report that the average home movie scene should run about 10 seconds in length, it isn't quite so easy to dispel the sinister overtones trailing along behind.

SINISTER OVERTONE A: That there's a faint aroma of the stopwatch in this moviemaking business. Actually, not so. Anyone playing around with a movie camera has enough on his mind while merely attending to correct exposure and keeping up with his subject to preclude any faint possibility that he might also do a bit of timekeeping on the side. Anyway, it just isn't necessary.

SINISTER OVERTONE B: That, since the average scene should last for about 10 seconds, *all* scenes should be 10 seconds long. Emphatically, not so. Aside from the outright monotony of it, this would be rather like buying a half dozen size 7 dungarees for a family of six children and then altering the pants to each child's individual requirements.

An individual movie scene should be exactly as long as it needs to be. If the person or persons you are photographing are doing something interesting, keep your finger on the camera button until they cease to be interesting or until your shooting distance ceases to be the best one. If the action demands a closer shot or a farther one, stop shooting and shift position.

CONTINUITY AT WORK

This story tells itself. When the activity shifts from a lesson to story-reading or then to snack time, you see what's going on. Notice how much the close-ups contribute. The pictures were made on Kodak Tri-X, a film that permits owners of 16mm cameras to shoot indoor movies without a light bar.

111

Unfortunately, this is rather like telling a new bride how to compound a tricky pie filling entirely in terms of bits and pinches, when she's still not even certain how many teaspoonfuls make a tablespoon. About the only means of offering quantitative help is to say that very, very few scenes should ever be any briefer than 5 seconds; and equally few, any longer than 15. A film having lots of short scenes tends to seem spasmodic and jerky, while one in which the scenes are all long will drag.

The most entertaining movie is usually one in which there's considerable variety in scene length, with short scenes following long scenes, and with each individual scene lasting just long enough to contribute its special piece of action. Generally, there's enough natural variety in the length of time that chunks of activity last to provide this automatically.

You and your movie camera might, on some bright day, be off on a hike with a group of Campfire Girls who were just about to build, of all things, a campfire. The girls start bringing wood to some chosen location and you stand back with your camera to shoot this. After about 10 or 12 seconds, this parade of branch and stick bearers just starts to seem pretty repetitive, so you stop. You might, then, come in closer and shoot some footage of the girl who's arranging the fuel in regulation campfire style, probably for not more than 8 or 10 seconds because that's all it requires to show quite well what she's up to. If you want a close-up of her applying flaming match to kindling, chances are that this little scene wouldn't last more than 5 seconds. The action is an extremely brief one, and that's all you'd need to capture it satisfactorily.

Occasionally, a few very brief scenes can be used advantageously to get a feeling of fast pace in certain sorts of movies. If you were making a film of two small boys poking away at each other with boxing gloves, a linking of brief close-ups of gloves making contact with chins, faces, and noses would make the action seem even more furious than it probably was.

Many beginners have a tendency to shoot extremely lengthy scenes merely because they are afraid that, if they stop, they'll miss something important. It's possible that this might happen, but the danger of wasting great amounts of film and turning out tedious movies greatly overbalances it.

What's happening determines to a great degree the length of each scene. The initial one here might be fairly long and the second short or vice versa, just so they demonstrate that the boy is building a jump for his Flying Saucer. The third scene could be of medium length, but number four (which starts where the fourth picture does and ends at the fifth) must last as long as the action. For comic effect, the last scene would be a rather brief one.

Chapter X

Telephoto
and
Wide-Angle Lenses

COMMON AUXILIARY LENSES
for 8mm and 16mm cameras

Lens Types	Lenses for 8mm Cameras		Lenses for 16mm Cameras	
	Focal Length	Magni-fication	Focal Length	Magni-fication
Extra Wide-Angle	6.5mm	.5	12.5mm	.5
Wide-Angle	9mm	.7	15mm	.6
Normal	13mm	1	25mm	1
Telephoto	25mm	2	50mm	2
Super Telephoto	38mm or longer	3+	63mm or longer	2.5+

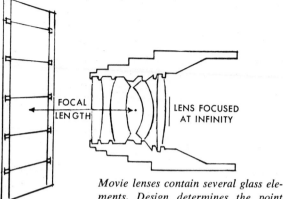

FOCAL LENGTH

LENS FOCUSED AT INFINITY

Movie lenses contain several glass elements. Design determines the point from which focal length is measured.

The Significance of Focal Length

All movie cameras have at least one lens, but one isn't necessarily a limit. Auxiliary lenses or lens converters are made for nearly every current model. Though you remain in the same position, they can whisk you close to distant action or shift you farther away from subjects so near or so large that they don't fit into your viewfinder.

The effect of an auxiliary lens or lens converter can be predicted by comparing its focal length with that of the lens normally used on the camera. Focal length is the distance from a certain part of the lens to the film when the lens is focused on infinity. It nearly always will be marked, either in millimeters or inches, somewhere on the lens mount. If the focal length is greater than that of the camera's normal lens (12 mm or 13 mm for 8mm cameras, 25 mm for 16mm cameras), the auxiliary lens or lens converter will be a telephoto. Most telephoto lenses are not real telescopes but merely have a narrower field of view than lenses of normal focal length. Since this narrower field of view fills the entire area of each movie frame, the result is similar to a telescope. A wide-angle lens has a shorter focal length and a wider field of view than a normal lens. This enables it to include a greater area on each frame of film and, since objects will register smaller, makes everything seem farther away.

This is a subject as you would see it through the viewfinder of a Brownie Movie Camera, Turret Model. The innermost rectangle shows the area covered by the telephoto lens, the middle ring the normal lens, and the outer ring the wide-angle lens.

The wide-angle lens includes the greatest area, in this instance about 50 percent more than the normal lens.

The normal lens is a practical compromise between the wide-angle's great covering power and the telephoto's distance-shrinking ability.

The telephoto gives the effect of decreasing camera-to-subject distance, by two-thirds over the wide-angle, by one-half over the normal lens.

Whether you'd like to show one solitary little bird or a screen full of them, there's a movie lens available that will make the job easier. A telephoto lens or lens converter is ideal for photographing small subjects that can't be too closely approached on foot.

AREA COVERED BY LENSES OF DIFFERENT FOCAL LENGTH

16mm Cameras

Distance from Film to Subject in Feet	15mm				25mm				50mm				102mm			
	Width		Height		Width		Height		Width		Height		Width		Height	
	Ft.	In.	Ft.	In.	Ft.	In.	Ft.	In.	Ft.	In.	Ft.	In.	Ft.	In.	Ft.	In.
10	–	–	–	–	3	8½	2	9½	1	10½	1	5	–	10¾	–	8⅛
6	3	7	2	8¼	2	2½	2	7¾	1	1½	–	10⅛	–	6¼	–	4⅝
4	2	4½	1	9¼	1	5½	1	1	–	9	–	6¾	–	3¹⁵⁄₁₆	–	2¹⁵⁄₁₆
2	1	1¾	–	10⅜	–	8⅜	–	6	–	4⅜	–	3⅜	–	–	–	–

8mm Cameras

Distance from Film to Subject in Feet	9mm				12mm				25mm				38mm			
	Width		Height		Width		Height		Width		Height		Width		Height	
	Ft.	In.	Ft.	in.	Ft.	In.	Ft.	in.	Ft.	In.	Ft.	in.	Ft.	In.	Ft.	In.
10	4	7¾	3	6	3	5¼	2	7	1	8½	1	3¼	1	1¾	–	10⅜
6	2	9½	2	1¼	2	¾	1	6½	1	¼	–	9⅛	–	8¼	–	6⅛
4	1	10½	1	5	1	4½	1	½	–	8⅛	–	6⅛	–	5½	–	4⅛
2	–	11⅜	–	8⅝	–	8¼	–	6⅛	–	4	–	3	–	2⅝	–	2

The focal length of a lens or lens converter, by itself, tells nothing about whether it is a telephoto or a wide-angle device. A 19mm unit would, for example, be a telephoto on an 8mm camera and a wide-angle on a 16mm. The way of knowing its effect is a comparison with the focal length of the normal lens.

If the focal length of a telephoto lens is twice that of the normal lens, it has the effect of halving the camera-to-subject distance and making all objects in the picture appear twice as large as they'd be with the normal lens. When you mount a 100mm lens on a 16mm camera, the result would be about the same as if you had suddenly reduced the space between yourself and your subject by three-quarters.

If the focal length of a wide-angle lens is half that of the normal lens, it has the effect of doubling the camera-to-subject distance so that all objects appear only half as big as they would with the normal lens.

On many movie cameras, the normal lens is entirely removable and can be replaced by other lenses of different focal length. A great range of different focal-length lenses is available for both 8mm and 16mm equipment. Such cameras generally have adjustable viewfinders which can be set for lenses of many different focal lengths so that they provide an accurate view of the area being "seen" by the lens on the camera. It's extremely important that the viewfinder be set at the same focal length as the lens being used.

By means of optical gadgets called "lens converters," many cameras with lenses that are permanently fixed can still have much of the flexibility of those with removable lenses. These are devices which fit over the camera's fixed lens and change its viewpoint to that of either a telephoto or a wide-angle. For most cameras, only a single focal-length telephoto converter and a single focal-length wide-angle converter are made. With the converters are supplied masks which slide over the camera's regular viewfinder and mark out the field of view for that particular converter.

Turret-type cameras have two or three lenses or lens converters mounted on a wheel up front so that a change from normal to telephoto or any other switch can be made almost instantly with a single twist of the wrist.

To appreciate fully what a super-telephoto lens (one of 38mm or greater focal length for 8mm shooting, 63mm or greater for 16mm) can do, you must see actual movies made with one. At an exciting corrida you may be far up in the grandstand, but a super-telephoto puts your camera right behind the matador's shoulder.

A telephoto lens offers a special dividend when used for movies of nature subjects. It not only provides frame-filling close-ups but also creates an attractively out-of-focus background.

Nothing can keep you more effectively away from a prospective movie subject than bars. But a telephoto lens spans distance that you can't, makes it possible to shoot excellent zoo films.

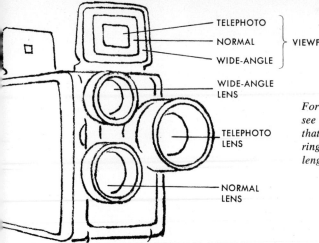

TELEPHOTO
NORMAL
WIDE-ANGLE
} VIEWFINDERS

WIDE-ANGLE LENS

TELEPHOTO LENS

NORMAL LENS

For the film and your eye to see the same area, it's vital that you use the viewfinder ring that matches the focal length of the lens being used.

How and When to Use a Telephoto

A telephoto lens is invaluable for making movies of subjects you can't get as close to as you might wish — spectator sports, birds and animals, planes and trains. It will help you capture wonderfully natural childhood activity, since you can shoot from far enough away so your quarry won't guess there's a camera anywhere in the vicinity.

With telephoto lenses of more than about three times the focal length of your camera's normal lens, it's rather difficult to get a really steady picture unless you use a tripod. Slight camera movement usually isn't evident in movies made with lenses of normal focal length but a telephoto will magnify it to the same degree as it magnifies the size of objects. Modern tripods are

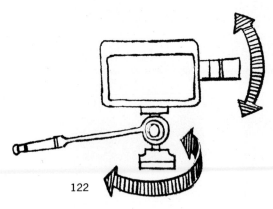

A tilting-turning tripod head not only permits the camera to move laterally and longitudinally, but also both ways at the same time.

light-weight and can be condensed into pocket-sized packages. For movie shooting, it's important to have one with a tilting-turning head device so that you can move your camera smoothly as you follow your subject. A tripod of this type will cost approximately twenty dollars.

In addition, telephoto lenses have a narrower range of sharp focus than lenses of normal focal length. Distance from camera to subject should be estimated with considerable care, especially for fairly close scenes. When extreme close-ups are photographed with a telephoto, it's essential to make an actual measurement.

Shooting with a Wide-Angle Lens

A wide-angle lens expands the indoors. With only a normal focal length lens you often discover that you can't get as much area into your scenes as you'd like. Either it's because a wall stops you from backing up any farther or because, when you're able to back up far enough, your photofloods are so far from the subject that you can't get a satisfactory exposure.

But, with a wide-angle lens or lens converter you can beat both problems. If you're back-to-wall and still don't have enough distance between you and your subject, a 9mm wide-angle lens on your 8mm camera has the effect of stretching that range by half-again more than it is. If you find that it takes a camera-to-subject distance of 20 feet to get subjects full length, but that your two-lamp light bar doesn't provide enough illumination, a wide-angle lens will include just as much area at 14 feet, from where the lamps do provide enough.

A wide-angle lens is also helpful outdoors for squeezing a large building or natural wonder into a movie frame. It also does a better job than the normal focal length lens when you shoot movies through the windshield of a moving vehicle.

One of the greatest advantages of having both wide-angle and telephoto lenses at your command is the marvelous variety they can provide for shooting films of sports events, outdoor entertainments, graduation ceremonies, or other situations when your own location is fixed. By switching from one lens to the other, your film will have a pleasant variety where it might otherwise seem dull and monotonous.

With a wide-angle lens you can cram a large area onto the film even when, as in a boat, you aren't able to move back any farther (top). It also helps exaggerate distance for effect (middle) and gives you nearly full-length views of people in rather small rooms.

Size and scope are a wide-angle lens' bread and butter. So many vast natural and man-made wonders would appear considerably less breath-taking than they are unless shown complete and whole in the movies shot of them. A wide-angle lens does this superlatively.

125

Chapter XI

Editing
and Titling

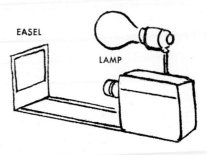

EASEL

LAMP

A movie titler presents your imagination with a willing sparring partner. Maps, photographs, a typewriter, printed illustrations, stick-on letters, and colored paper all become potential titling tools.

A complete editing outfit permits you to check your movie footage carefully yet easily, mark it for any subsequent cutting, make good solid splices, and wind it onto a single reel.

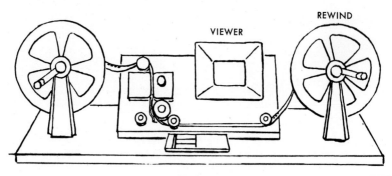

REWIND

VIEWER

SPLICER

Equipment for Editing and Titling

Editing, primitive style, can be performed with paraphernalia no more lavish than the splicing board for which plans appear on page 77. If you prefer to essay editing rather gingerly and especially if you already own a splicing rig, you'll be able to get along quite satisfactorily with it although at a rather pedestrian pace. For the utmost speed and convenience, though, there's no substitute for a specially designed editing outfit.

In a single package, these outfits offer the following components: a pair of rewinds; a projection device which shows your pictures on a small, built-in glass screen; a splicer; and a gadget you can use to nick the edge of the film as a mark for later cutting. Such units vary in price from about forty dollars to more than one hundred, with the price differences often attributable to differences in the size of the projection device.

A great deal of interesting titling can be done quite easily and without any special equipment by utilizing signs, markers, and other natural titles encountered on location. Ingenuity is also a valuable asset in title making. For a reel of beach activities you can create an effective title simply by photographing someone's finger writing in wet sand.

But, to reinforce all of the other titling media that are available, it's quite worth while to consider the potentialities of a full-fledged titling outfit. It will permit you to use maps, snapshot prints, typed or hand-lettered cards, color illustrations from books and magazines, special masks, and all sorts of trickery in your titles. A titler not only presents an almost endless challenge to your own inventiveness for purely titling work but can also be exploited for extreme close-up photography of flowers and other tiny subjects.

The Brownie Movie Titler Outfit is designed especially for the Brownie Movie Cameras and is sold for about fifteen dollars. Other titlers, adaptable to different cameras, are offered by several manufacturers at several prices. The most desirable include, as the Brownie does, a mount for the camera, a fixture for one or more lights, a versatile easel on which to locate the title material, and a close-up lens which, when placed in front of the camera's normal lens, allows it to get a sharp picture at the close camera-to-easel distance.

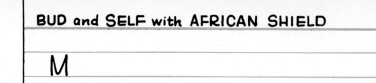

M

AN EXAMPLE OF EDITING
This is a scene card for editing a movie. The heading at the top identifies the scene. The "M" indicates it is a medium-distance scene. The remaining space would contain any corrective notes.

Imagine that each of the pictures here is a complete scene on a movie reel returned to you from the processing laboratory. The adjoining comments would be those written on your scene cards. To see the result of this editing, turn to pages 133 and 136.

BIT TOO LONG —
CUT OUT SOME OF
CONCLUDING FOOTAGE

TOO UNDER-EXPOSED —
CHOP OUT ENTIRELY

OK

CUT SOME EARLY
FOOTAGE SO TRAIN
EMERGES FROM TUNNEL
AS SCENE BEGINS

MOVE FARTHER FRONT
SO IT COMES <u>BEFORE</u>
FIRST VIEW OF TRAIN
AND BECOMES TITLE

OK

UNEXPOSED FILM FROM
TURNING REEL OVER FOR
SECOND RUN THROUGH
CAMERA — CHOP OUT

CUT OUT PART AT END
WHEN BUD LOOKS
AT CAMERA

CAMERA MOVED —
CHOP OUT ENTIRELY

OK

129

The Technique of Editing

The difference between mere splicing and editing is about the same as that between painting a house and painting a picture. Although the tools are pretty much the same, the approach to one is much more creative and sophisticated than to the other.

Editing is a cosmetic kind of treatment for home movies. Like any cosmetic, it can't transform basically poor original material into something artful and lovely. Even the wonders of photography aren't capable of turning the sow's-ear-to-silk-purse trick. But, with predominantly good original footage, it can perform a remarkable polishing job.

In the editing process, long scenes can be shortened to enhance the pace of the movie. Poorly focused, badly exposed, uninteresting, or irrelevant footage can be removed. Scenes can be rearranged in different order if the new order yields better continuity or a more interesting result. It's even possible to combine scenes made at different times and on different reels. Humorous footage can be chopped into short sections and inserted at various places in the movie to provide a running gag. And, when specially made titles are also added during editing, the result, depending upon the quality of the original reels and the imagination of the editor, can be pretty nearly the acme of home moviemaking.

Of course, a tremendous amount of editing can be done in the camera if you photograph activities in their normal sequence, include natural titles whenever possible, strive to avoid exposure and focusing errors, and work for natural continuity. The greater your success in doing these things, the more value you get from your investment in film. But if 90 percent of a reel is so good that you wouldn't want to alter it in any way (and 90 percent is an unusually high batting average), the additional ten percent might be so glaring to an audience of family and friends that it would overshadow the quality of the larger portion. It's hardly an exaggeration so say that almost every reel returned from a processing laboratory can become a better movie through some editing.

The process of editing is fun. It has much of the appeal for adults that pasting pictures into a scrap book has for kids. In fact, the similarity is great even though the editing materials

130

are somewhat more complex.

Some editing can be done almost like mental arithmetic. It merely involves running a reel of film through your editor, snipping out occasional dull or poorly photographed sections, rearranging one or two scenes, and adding a title at the beginning. In this sort of once-over-lightly editing, you can carry all the necessary ideas in your head and need never commit the intended organization of your movie to writing.

But full-scale editing requires more planning. To start, place yourself in a chair and the chair within arm's length of your projector. Make sure that there's a package of small file cards on the table in front of you and a pencil at hand.

Start the projector and make out a card for each individual scene by jotting down a few identifying words at the top of the card. If you have a preponderance of brief scenes, you may have to run the reel through more than once.

After you have made all the scene cards, project the film again. This time, make editing analysis notes on the cards. Indicate whether the scene is primarily a long-distance, medium-distance, or close-up one. If its content is exactly as you want it, mark a check on the card. If the scene is too long or if part of it has areas of fog from incorrect loading or if portions are out of focus or if exposure is poor or for any other reason it should be cut out, note that down, too. Before long you'll probably develop a handy code.

Once you've finished this analysis, add scene cards for any scenes on other reels of film that logically belong with those on the reel you've just looked at. Often scenes made at different times fit together quite neatly. Doing this isn't cheating. The entire idea of editing, after all, is to assemble an interesting movie, not necessarily a chronologically exact record.

If you're putting together a vacation film, you might have three, four, or even more sets of scene cards from as many individual reels shot during the course of your travels. You might also have made some special titles on a separate reel. Add the cards for all of these together into one big stack.

Now arrange the cards in the order you think most interesting. As you do this, remember that you'll be doing some cutting, as indicated by the comments on the cards. This phase of

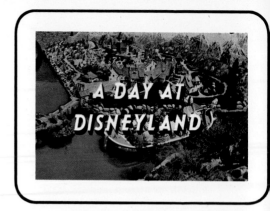

A DAY AT DISNEYLAND

This is a home movie story that has been edited. How the editing was performed on a portion of it is shown on pages 128 and 129. Also, though, it is an example of the manner in which the presence of just a few titles can enhance any home movie. In this instance we have a "manufactured" title at the very beginning and several natural titles farther along. All of these titles fall into place quite unobtrusively and, in a sense, assume the role performed in a book by chapter headings. They not only break up the over-all story into smaller, more digestible chunks, but also, and perhaps even more important, they serve to introduce new settings and new activities. Note how, in this as in all of the other complete movie stories shown earlier in the book, the frequent use of attractive close-ups makes a valuable contribution.

132

The Santa Fe and Disneyland R.R. must be one of the busiest lines in the world, so . . .

. . . when our train chugged into the old-fashioned terminal . . .

. . . we didn't waste any time in getting aboard one of the coaches.

It brought us quickly from the everyday world into the amazing and magical world of Disneyland.

It seemed like a good idea to get properly togged out . . .

. . . so we looked into the headgear situation. It was an especially hard choice for Bud . . .

. . . and he finally ended up by wheedling three out of me.

Nearby we ran into a display of shields and he'd have liked a couple of them, too.

133

Continued on page 136

editing is the one in which you should drop out the cards representing scenes either too weak photographically or too irrelevant for your final movie.

In shuffling these cards, you needn't be guided strictly by the chronological order in which events really occurred. If some other order seems reasonable and more interesting, use it. On a vacation trip, you might have spent the first and second days sightseeing and the third day swimming. Just for variety, it probably would be better to insert the swimming sequences between the two groups of scenic material.

As you arrange and rearrange your scene cards, keep striving for natural continuity and check your markings of subject distance so you don't, inadvertently, link together extensive chains of either all long-distance scenes or close-ups. When you finally get the order that appeals to you most, consider whether any special titles might be advantageous in certain spots. Returning to the example of a vacation film, if you were showing a trip during which you visited two or three national parks and stayed at a couple of memorable lodges, it might be worthwhile to have a title for each park and lodge to precede the scenes showing them.

Once you have *all* your film at hand, both original footage and special titles, and all of your scene cards representing them, number the cards consecutively from the top of the pile down. At this point you'll find it especially handy to have a unique piece of editing equipment, strictly homemade. Get one or two metal wastepaper baskets. Out of scraps, make a wooden "T," the upright two to three feet high and the crossbar about as wide as the waste basket. Nail a row of ordinary brads into the crossbar with a quarter-inch of each sticking out. If you shoot 8mm film, place the brads about a half-inch apart. Number the brads consecutively from left to right. If you make two of these gadgets, and it's an especially good idea to have two for 16mm editing, begin numbering the brads on the second where you left off with those on the first. Then bolt each upright to the back of a waste-paper basket.

Next, run through the editor each reel of film containing scenes for your movie. Place a nick at the beginning and end of every scene you plan to use and cut the scenes apart at the nick

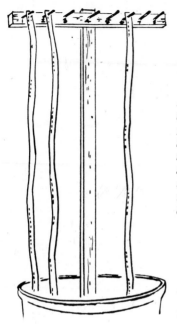

A film editing "T" is simply what it appears to be, a wooden "T" fastened to a waste paper basket. Small brads should be nailed into the horizontal member and spaced far enough apart so that strips of film can be hung from them. It's helpful if the brads are numbered consecutively.

marks. If two or more scenes follow each other on both the original reels and the cards, however, there's no need to cut them apart. As you remove each scene, hang it by its top perforation from the brad having the same number as its card. It's advisable to wear a pair of inexpensive white cotton gloves while you are handling the film. When several scenes are connected together, hang them from the number of the first scene on the strip, but leave vacant the brads marked with the numbers of the others. The tails of the film can hang down into the basket.

When this is done, the scenes will be in the same order as their cards. Simply edit the individual lengths of film as indicated by your comments on the cards and, once you've finished this, splice them together, starting at number one. Be careful, though, not to cinch the film tight on its reel, since this can scratch it severely.

Continued from page 133

Although we'd done a little railroading already, we didn't want to miss . . .

. . . a ride behind Casey Jones and his steam calliope.

The route was really tremendous, complete with tunnel "carved" out of solid rock.

Even the most enthusiastic sight-seers need some sustenance . . .

. . . and Bud tackled a hamburger just about as big as the boy.

Karen did all right, too.

The kids decided that they'd been earthbound long enough, so . . .

. . . they chose to climb aboard an airborne elephant.

There's Karen. She's wondering whether it mightn't have been a good idea to take a parachute.

A little later on we found an old-time ice cream cart.

Naturally, this had considerable attraction to the small fry.

And, as you can guess, they were less than overjoyed when we had to head for home.

Ways, Means, and Ideas for Titling

For a moment, transplant yourself from behind the projector out into one of your home-movie audiences. Let's say that the screen is bustling with scenes of the kids at the zoo. You can see them clambering up onto a fence and craning for a better view. Then there's a close-up of their delighted faces, then the aquatic gymnastics of the sea lions who are entertaining them, then Mom in the midst of a kaleidoscope of pansies.

The effect is a lot like shifting suddenly from a forward gear into reverse. If the screech isn't aural, it's certainly mental. You can explain the abrupt transition by mentioning aloud that, after touring the zoo, you walked over to the botanical gardens, but this still doesn't eliminate the basic awkwardness.

The neatest means of handling a situation like this would simply have been to aim the camera at the sign identifying the gardens and shoot about five seconds' worth of film before making any other scenes there. This would have created a title, and titles are the best introductions and transitions. They need be no more complex than this one.

Fortunately for home moviemakers, the landscape is liberally dotted with prospective title material erected by states, municipalities, park commissions, historical societies, highway departments, and commercial enterprises. Ships' life preservers are good titles. So are the names painted on airliners. To shoot this kind of title, just get as close as your camera and the situation will permit and keep the button pressed down for about twice as long as is needed to read the printing slowly. No title, however, should ever be briefer than about five seconds.

Should you lack a ready-made title, ingenuity can often move mountains. A movie tour of a garden might be introduced by an over-the-shoulder view of some seed packets being held by the gardener. Indoors, you'll discover that items as simple as a child's blackboard, alphabet blocks, or anagram letters can be used advantageously. If you're planning to shoot some local festival, a newspaper with a banner headline announcing it makes a fine title. A birthday cake, all by itself, is a wonderful title, one that can have a little extra action added by having someone outside the picture area blow out the candles while you're shooting.

Occasionally, you can even shoot a special introduction to the title, itself. For a family fishing expedition you might make a brief scene of the youngest fisherman in your brood proudly holding a large fish while Dad, displaying something about the size of a runt sardine, glowers. In editing, this scene could be placed just before the highway marker giving the name of the lake. To precede some first films of a newborn baby, you might shoot some male feet pacing back and forth across the floor until, suddenly, they stop and a pair of female feet in white shoes appears in the picture. Then the actual title, an open box of cigars with a small sign giving vital statistics pinned to it, could follow.

There's nothing at all tricky about this sort of titling. These are ordinary movie scenes which can be shot at any time and later spliced into another reel. The important ingredient is imagination.

With titling equipment, such as the Brownie Movie Titler Outfit and some of the other titlers available in camera shops, you can transform a magazine illustration, a color snapshot, a map, a picture postcard, or even a travel folder into a colorful title. Some of these will probably be complete in themselves and can go into the titler as is. Others will require the addition of some form of text.

The text portion of any title should be kept as brief as possible, no longer than eight to ten words. One of the most readily available and versatile instruments for preparing text is a typewriter, since it can print on wallpaper, poster paper, the light areas of a photographic print, and numerous other surfaces. For dark, sharp titles, the typewriter's ribbon should be new or nearly new.

Another easy way of engineering text material is via the ceramic and wooden letters sold in sets by many photo shops. These can be fastened to a background card or picture with double-coated cellophane tape.

Should you own any skill with pen or brush, it can be exercised profitably in the production of home movie titles. Start with a rectangle of cardboard or colored paper, just so long as it's the size required for your titler, and let your ingenuity run unchecked. If it's a challenge to you to draw a reasonably

TITLES UNLIMITED

Just about everywhere that you and your movie camera go there are natural titles on hand, free for the taking. Sometimes they'll be quite conventional, such as road signs or historical markers; sometimes, though, they may be as unique and interesting as the place they describe. The "Bears and Barbed Wire" sign is an excellent example. Here is a small sampler of natural titles merely to demonstrate the enormous variety of title material available.

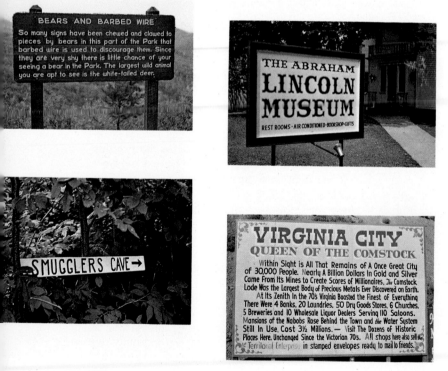

LIFE IN THE AQUARIUM

With a titler, a small sheet of clear plastic material, and some plastic letters you can create live titles like this one quite easily.

straight line, you may find it entirely within your artistic capabilities to make wonderfully colorful titles with scissors and paste. First, cut a rectangle of colored paper of the size used by your titler. This will be the background. Then merely cut some simple shapes out of other colors to form either a design or a simple picture, paste them on the background, type the text material, and shoot.

Since titlers can also be used for ultra close-up moviemaking (see page 170), this presents some additional titling possibilities. You might, for instance, cut a sheet of clear rigid plastic to the dimensions of your titler easel and place a few words on it, either by inking them in or with movable letters. This can then be mounted in the titler and some flowers, a kitten's face, a mounted butterfly, or some fish swimming in an aquarium placed directly behind it. When this sort of titling is done, it's especially important for the titler to be held steady.

Actually, the greatest pitfall of titling is that, once you start doing it, the process may become so engrossing that you'll tend to overload your films with title material. Titles should be employed only to introduce movies and to explain things about them that aren't self-apparent. The movie, itself, should still be the chief attraction.

Running Gags and "Orphaned" Film

Editing and titling, then, are post-shooting methods of smoothing out your movies, making them more intelligible, enhancing their continuity. There aren't any strict rules for good editing or good titling, only methods. Just as everyone will film a certain event in a different way, everyone edits and titles to the tune of his own taste, patience, and capabilities.

Although most editing and titling is done to improve some sort of natural story that already exists on one or more reels of film, both can be used to accomplish even more.

They can, for example, furnish a liberal helping of humor. You might be filming a Saturday's activities around the house. Perhaps someone has acquired a new car, and his tender loving care of it has become something of a family joke. If you can catch this person out washing or polishing his pride-and-joy, shoot one extremely long scene of his labor of love. Then, instead of using the film all together, insert brief chunks of it in four or five different breaks between sequences entirely unrelated to it. You might precede each with a title like, "Meanwhile, back at the driveway . . ." This is called a "running gag," and there are endless variations of the technique. Mac Sennett and his contemporaries used them hilariously, and time hasn't dulled their potentialities.

Editing also permits the linking of short "orphaned" sequences that, while interesting in themselves, don't really fit into an extensive movie story. Any pair of parents who make movies of their small fry is likely to have a good deal of this sort of footage languishing around. You can make marvelous growing-up reels of children with such film by merely arranging a collection of scenes in chronological order so that, over a period of four or five minutes, you'll be able to watch a son or daughter progress from a newborn infant through all the fascinating stages of childhood. In this sort of movie, only an introductory title is essential. The movie tells its own story.

When an especially good humor and titling mood sieze you simultaneously, you can often get quite funny results out of other "orphaned" film by editing it into a comic newsreel. A title like "Great medical discovery announced" might precede a few scenes of the kids playing doctor. "New production records set" might introduce your cat or dog surrounded by a large and bustling litter. "Opportunities for computing machines" might present some sequences of a golfer having a difficult time getting out of a sandtrap. This sort of material can be linked together until you run out of film or out of bright ideas.

DOING IT YOURSELF
Homemade "manufactured" movie titles needn't be just letters lined up against a colored background. The most unlikely-seeming materials may help you create the most successful titles. For example, the interesting texture in "Flowers In Our Garden" comes from children's finger paints.

There's nothing more to this kind of title than a photographic color print of your favorite youngster and some wooden or plastic letters. For a way of animating the letters, see page 176.

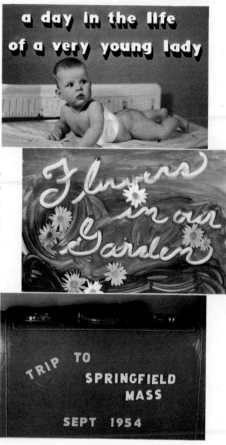

The background was created with finger paints on waxed paper. It was placed on a concrete walk in bright sun and, as the camera ground away, someone dropped the blossoms, one at a time.

Flexible plastic letters will adhere to almost any fairly smooth surface without glue. In this instance the surface is the side of a suitcase, since it emphasizes the travel idea.

This title consists of triangles of colored paper, wooden letters, and a couple of carnations. Such titles can be laid out on the floor and photographed with your light bar attached to the camera.

On a card of the size required by a movie titler, the text was "printed" in a typewriter. The artwork was then simply cut from sheets of colored paper and pasted down for filming in the titler.

With the camera shooting down at the floor, its light bar attached, various printed souvenirs of New York City were dropped, one at a time, to create a pleasantly informal pattern.

Many varied materials can be employed as backgrounds for wooden or plastic letters. Wood and wallpaper are two interesting possibilities. Here a portion of a matchstick bamboo drape was used.

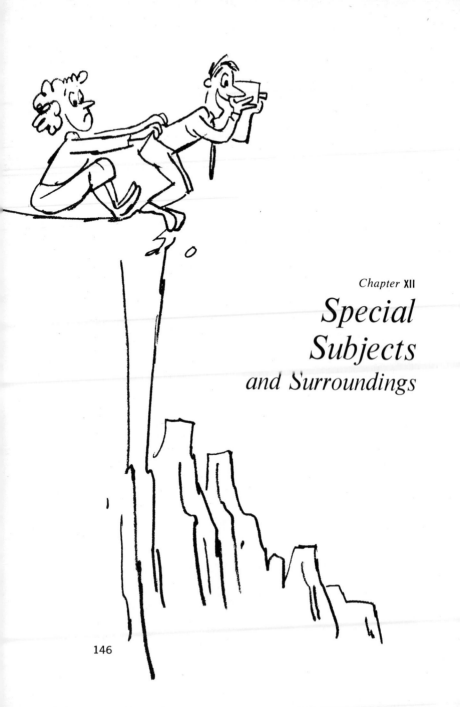

Chapter **XII**

Special Subjects

and Surroundings

RAINBOWS: Use the same lens setting recommended for an average subject in bright sunlight (8 with Kodachrome Film, Daylight Type), unless conditions are cloudy. In that case, try a setting halfway between 5.6 and 8.

SILHOUETTES: A silhouette results when there's a background much more brightly lighted than anything in the foreground and the lens setting is based entirely on photographing that background. All that's in the foreground turns out entirely black in the picture and therefore stands out against the relatively light, colorful background. In moviemaking, silhouettes are especially dramatic in scenes of sunsets and sunrises. A building, a rock formation, or any other object outlined against the multicolored sky adds a feeling of third dimension. Even better, if you can get some people silhouetted against the sky, especially if they are moving about to do something, it will provide your sunset or sunrise scene with a real movie character.

Nearly all of this data is condensed in the *Kodak Movie Photoguide,* the pocket-sized compendium of movie-shooting information sold by most camera shops.

SUNSETS AND SUNRISES: Exposure isn't especially critical. Even if the colors in your movie aren't an exact match for those in the scene, they'll still be quite breathtaking. Don't shoot directly

147

Nature presents its sunsets in a virtually limitless variety of hues and effects. Most of them are warmly drawn in reds, oranges, and yellows, but occasionally, as above, one can be equally spectacular when consisting solely of blues. Note how, in two of these scenes, the foreground objects have become silhouetted. This occurs because the lens opening has been set in terms of the lighter area behind them. The scene at the lower right demonstrates that a good sunset sequence can be made merely by showing how the sun's colors and shadows paint the surrounding landscape.

toward the sun until it slips behind clouds or is sufficiently obscured so that you can look at it without discomfort. Since objects in the foreground will be greatly underexposed, they'll appear as silhouettes.

Fifteen minutes before sunset or after sunrise (both times are announced daily by local weather bureaus), try a lens setting of 5.6 with Kodachrome Film; five minutes before sunset or after sunrise, a setting of 4; right at sunset and sunrise, 2.8. If you'd like to capture some of the afterglow or preglow, set your lens at its largest opening.

LIGHT SAND AND SNOW SCENES: If the lens setting recommended for average subjects in bright sunlight is used in photographing this kind of scenery, the film will turn out extremely light due to overexposure. This occurs because the scene probably contains nearly all light colors rather than the usual distribution of light and dark ones. For well-exposed Kodachrome movies, then, it's necessary to set the lens at 11. If there are people in the foreground, though, whose activities are the chief source of interest in your movie, expose with the lens set halfway between 8 and 11.

When there's a bright sun shining on light sand or snow, the lens setting for a scene such as the one at the left should be 11. If there are people in the near foreground, though, the setting with Kodachrome Film should be halfway between 8 and 11.

These conditions also tend to fool exposure meters, and should you attempt to obtain the lens setting with a reflected light meter used in the conventional manner, it would probably report a lens opening too small and therefore result in dark, underexposed movies. Again, the unusual sameness of colors rather than a normal proportion of light and dark ones is the cause. For better results, take your meter reading from the palm of your hand and use it directly.

Many desert areas of the Southwest are strewn with colorful rock formations or interesting vegetation. For these, the lens setting should also be halfway between 8 and 11.

WATERFALLS AND SURF: Both seem to move faster in movies than in actuality, especially when photographed from fairly close range. If your camera offers you a choice of speeds, shoot waterfalls and surf at 32 frames per second; under bright sunlight, the lens setting for Kodachrome Film, Daylight Type, should be halfway between 5.6 and 8. For movies made at 16 frames per second in bright sunlight, use a lens setting halfway between 8 and 11.

FOG: In dense fog with sunlight overhead but not breaking through, shoot at 2.8 with Kodachrome Film, Daylight Type. A thin fog is about the same as cloudy bright, so the lens setting for it should be 4.

A low-hanging fog usually brings an eery and mysterious quality along with it. The colors in your movies will be thin and rather faint pastel versions of their normal, sunlighted hues.

In deep shade with no open sky overhead, an exposure meter is the only sure guide to the correct lens setting. If you have none, try 1.9.

IN SHADE: In deep woods, under a porch roof, or with some other object shading your subject from the overhead light of the sky, the lens opening for Kodachrome Film, Daylight Type, must be at least as large as 1.9 on a clear, sunny day. Even this will be something of a gamble. For situations like this, an exposure meter is the only means of being sure about your lens setting. Since the light in shaded areas is extremely blue, a Kodak Skylight Filter over the lens will give a more pleasing picture by eliminating some of this bluishness.

AT HIGH ELEVATIONS: The sun isn't brighter in mountainous country than at sea level, but the scenery is. Mountain views consist largely of sky and of distant objects partially obscured by light blue haze. With Kodachrome Film, Daylight Type, use a lens setting halfway between 8 and 11. A Kodak Skylight Filter (No. 1A) over the lens will minimize the haze and not affect the lens setting. When shooting movies of people in mountainous surroundings, use the same settings you'd use anywhere else.

A storm proper isn't nearly as good movie material as its onset. The contrast of a still sunlit landscape with the oncoming thunderclouds makes for first rate drama.

Flashing electric signs or their reflections are among the most spectacular movie subjects. To shoot color - illuminated fountains, set your lens at its widest opening.

Atmospheric conditions in mountainous country can vary from extremely hazy to crisp and clear. A Skylight filter will greatly help in minimizing haze, affect scenes made on clear days only slightly.

RAINSTORMS OR BLIZZARDS: Do your shooting from some protected location where rain or snow cannot get on your lens and blur the pictures. A light rainfall calls for a lens setting of 2.8, but, for a heavier storm with dark clouds overhead, try 1.9. Movies of most snowstorms can be made on Kodachrome Film, Daylight Type, with the lens set at 4. Over-all scenes of falling snow and rain seldom look as real as you might wish them to. For better effects, shoot raindrops spattering in puddles or snowflakes falling in front of a dark doorway.

FIREWORKS AND ELECTRIC SIGNS: Kodachrome Film, Type A, accentuates the reds, oranges, and yellows that usually predominate in these subjects. However, both Type A and Daylight Type films can be used quite satisfactorily. Shoot bright bursts of fireworks fairly near the camera at a lens setting of 2.8. Less brilliant bursts or more distant ones will require a setting of 1.9 or 1.4. Conventional electric signs and neon signs can be photographed at 2.8. For night fires and campfires, try a setting of 1.9. People near the fires will appear in your movies as silhouettes.

Animated signs, the spectaculars often encountered in entertainment centers like Times Square, Las Vegas, and the Chicago Loop, are especially good movie subjects. Shoot them at 2.8.

Chapter XIII

Special Occasions

Movies from the Air

Whenever you go aloft, your movie camera can go right along with you and spark your travel films with some breath-taking aerial footage. Except for a slight difference in lens settings required at high altitudes, the mechanics are almost exactly the same as those for moviemaking on the ground.

From a seat up front in an airliner's cabin you can catch the slow turning over of the propeller until, with a cough of smoke, the engine finally takes hold. Then you'll be able to show the blurred landscape racing by at an ever increasing rate until the plane lifts off the runway. For this scene, it's a good idea to keep the edge of the plane's wing and, perhaps, one of its engines along the side of your picture as a sort of frame.

Once you're well up in the air, there'll be checkerboards of plowed fields to shoot, rivers and lakes, dams, bridges, highway systems and their complex intersections, factories, mountains, and shore lines. When you approach some especially noted natural wonder, chances are that the stewardess will give you some advance notice so that you can have your camera ready. Aerial views of Niagara Falls, of the Grand Canyon, or the Continental Divide have a scope incomparably greater than anything you might shoot on the ground.

If you're on your way to tour some large city, shoot as much of it as you can when the plane begins its approach to its airport. This kind of footage, especially when the city has the

LENS SETTINGS FOR AERIAL MOVIES WITH KODACHROME FILM, DAYLIGHT TYPE, EXPOSED AT 16 FRAMES-PER-SECOND

Altitude in Feet	Bright Sun	Hazy Sun	Cloudy Bright (Below Clouds)	Cloudy Dull (Below Clouds)
Below 2000	8	5.6	4	2.8
2000-4000	8-11	No Exposure Compensation for Altitude Necessary on Hazy or Cloudy Days.		
4000 and Over	11			
Above Clouds	11-16			

When aloft, you can accumulate memorable footage by aiming your camera either out or down. For the clearest, brightest possible colors in all of your aerial movie shooting, though, it's advisable to keep a filter like the Kodak Skylight Filter over the lens as a means of minimizing the effect of bluish haze.

aerial distinctiveness of a New York, a Washington, a San Francisco, a London, or a Paris, will make an excellent introduction to your land based coverage.

The higher your aerial vantage point, the greater the influence on exposure of the thin, blue haze always in the air. At altitudes below about 2,000 feet, your settings on a bright sunny day can be the same as you'd use on the ground. At higher altitudes, the lens opening should be smaller. The table on the previous page provides complete recommendations. To reduce the bluishness this haze causes in airborne color movies, keep a Kodak Skylight Filter over the camera lens.

Be sure that your camera is not directly touching a window or any other part of the aircraft because such contact will transmit to it the plane's vibrations. Unless you are purposely attempting to show the ground moving by at a rapid rate, as you might in scenes of the actual take-off or landing, it's desirable to shoot low altitude movies at 24 or 32 frames per second, since this has the effect of slowing the plane down and providing a better look at the ground. At extremely high altitudes it may be necessary to use a telephoto lens for a really interesting, fairly close-seeming view of something down below.

Weddings

A wedding can be a lovely color movie — one which the participants, their families, and friends will enjoy increasingly through the subsequent years. But there are two especially irritating anomalies about making a wedding film, and both should be weighed well before the wedding date.

The first is that the most difficult part of the entire bridal pageant to include in the movie is the very heart of it, the actual ceremony. Few churches and synagogues, even on the sunniest of days, are filled with enough daylight or a combination of daylight and artificial illumination so that color movies of people are possible. This can be checked by an exposure meter. In the occasional building that does receive sufficient light, due either to the size of its windows, its physical orientation, or the time of day, it's desirable to make your meter reading from the light reflected by your own hand, since accurate rendition of skin tones is probably more important than anything else. If most of the light enters through the windows, be sure to use

Kodachrome Film, Daylight Type, or Type A film with a daylight conversion filter over the lens.

Under any circumstances, the question of how much, if any, of the ceremony should be photographed must be decided by the bride, groom, and minister. Even if the illumination is sufficient for color movies, the central participants may prefer to dispense with the possible distraction of a movie camera. If the natural light isn't strong enough for ordinary moviemaking, the only alternative is the use of a photo light bar, and, to many couples, this may be even more objectionable. Should they desire films made during the taking of the marriage vows, select one vantage point, preferably during the wedding rehearsal, and do all of your shooting from there. In this way, you reduce the distraction to an absolute minimum.

Many couples who might not wish photofloods used around the altar won't object to their being used for movie scenes of the processional and recessional. You can fill in between these scenes with a view of the church interior with the wedding party at the altar. This can be shot from the rear, with the camera lens set at its largest opening.

The other major hurdle in making a wedding film is that too many things are usually going on at the same time. If you'd like to catch the groom and his best man arriving at the church, you may miss photographing the soloist. If you're specifically asked to shoot the ceremony, you won't be well located for the recessional. The best way to handle too much activity and too few of you is by planning and editing. At the rehearsal, for example, ask for the minister, the soloist, and the organist to don their robes so that you can photograph them close-up.

Shoot the organist's hands on the keys, with the sheet music in front of them. All of this footage, later on, can be spliced into the real wedding action and will greatly amplify it. Not everything can be shot in advance, but, by doing as much of this as possible, you'll include a great many integral ingredients of the wedding that might otherwise be missed.

If you have the time and the co-operation of the participants, a wedding movie can be wonderfully complete and include such preliminaries as trying on the gown and veil, opening gifts, posing for portraits, the rehearsal, and any prenuptial parties.

On the wedding day, you might be able to shoot the bride's and groom's preparations and their arrivals at the church. In all of this filming, work at getting plenty of close-ups of the members of the wedding party, of the families, even of the flowers. After the ceremony photograph the receiving line in the church vestibule, the gauntlet of rice run by the newly married couple, the parade of cars leaving the church, and, of course, the reception. Here, be certain to catch the toast to the bride, the cutting of the cake, the throwing of the bouquet, and the final getaway. Include as many of the guests as possible.

For title material, a close-up of either the actual wedding invitation or one of the newspaper stories of the wedding will serve nicely.

Since it's more than likely that you'll have a potpourri of both outdoor and indoor scenes in a wedding coverage, this is one of the instances when it's especially advantageous to do all the shooting on Kodachrome Film, Type A, and place a Kodak Daylight Filter for Kodak Type A Color Films over the lens outdoors. Daylight exposure settings for this combination are the same as those recommended for Daylight Type film.

Indoor Movies of Shows

Kodachrome movies of well-lighted theatrical events like ice shows, circuses, and professional plays are usually well within the capabilities of most home movie cameras and can be particularly excellent if you have a telephoto lens at your command. You should make sure, however, that the management has no objection to moviemaking.

In this kind of shooting, an exposure meter is pretty nearly useless. The meter cell "sees" a much wider area than that in which the performance occurs. Since most of this area is a good deal darker than the portion you're interested in photographing, the meter would lead you to believe that you could not shoot movies. If your target is something like a solo skater or dancer encased in the brilliance of a single spotlight, the meter may not provide any reading at all.

Kodachrome Film, Type A, is generally preferable to Daylight Type for such movie shooting, since the lights are more likely to approximate the warmth of the photoflood lamps for

An ice show is a festival of color, a whirlwind of action. Most scenes are brightly enough lighted so that they can be photographed on Kodachrome Film, preferably Type A. Try a setting of 2.8 when the subject is illuminated by a white spotlight, 1.9 when the spotlight is a pale color, and 1.4 when it is dark-colored.

which it is balanced than the cooler daylight.

For a subject isolated in several white spotlights, try a setting of 2.8, regardless of distance. When the spotlights are a color other than white but still a light color, use 1.9. A setting of 1.4 will probably be required when the spotlight is a dark color. When the performance is lighted over-all with white lights, a setting of 1.9 is advisable. Dimly lighted scenes or scenes illuminated with colored lights should be exposed at 1.4.

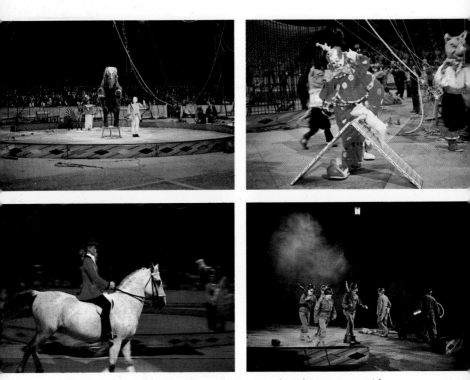

An event like a circus combines elaborate, colorful panoramas with exciting or funny pinpointed action. The ability to call on a wide-angle and a telephoto lens is a great aid if you hope to produce a color movie including scenes with large areas of pageantry and also scenes that close in on entertaining individual activity.

Most indoor sports and nearly all outdoor night sports are not lighted brightly enough for the taking of good color movies with Kodachrome Film. In some arenas which present hockey and basketball, the illumination is sufficient for shooting at a setting of 1.9 or 1.4.

For other indoor situations that you'd like to shoot by the existing light, it's pretty nearly essential to have an exposure meter since guesswork is quite fallible.

Movies for Sports and Business

As a medium for sports self-appraisal, nothing really compares with a movie, especially one exposed at slow motion speed. When the camera is operated at 32 or 64 frames per second, every small flaw in form becomes readily apparent. Best of all, you can view the film over and over again, then correct what needs correcting.

This is a method that's been in operation for many years by most college and high school coaches, particularly for football. Even night games can be photographed with 16mm equipment and Kodak Tri-X Reversal Film. A lens setting of 2.8 will do the job nicely at most high school stadiums.

In the field of civic activities, movies can provide a marvelous means of showing at money-raising time just what community agencies are doing with their funds. In industry, they are extraordinarily useful in fields as widely divergent as time-and-motion study and public relations. For detailed data on industrial applications, see the Kodak Data Book, *Industrial Motion Pictures,* sold by many photographic dealers.

When You Travel Abroad

When you tread on foreign soil, many things change abruptly, but none of them alter the motions you go through to make a good movie. You still use the same lens settings, still squeeze the same button, still crank up the spring motor after every scene.

The differences you'll encounter will be largely differences in supplying yourself with movie film and arranging to have that film processed. Customs regulations governing the amount of film you may carry duty-free from one country to another aren't entirely uniform, and individual customs officers often exercise considerable latitude in interpreting them. A friendly, co-operative attitude on your part in your relations with customs authorities can often move mountains.

If you're planning a junket on the continent, you'll find much pertinent and helpful data in the Kodak booklet, *Vacation Europe With Your Color Camera,* sold by most camera shops.

Here are a few basic considerations which may influence the photographic logistics for any trip you plan:

162

- *All Kodak film, particularly color film, is likely to be more expensive outside the United States. Kodachrome Movie Film sold abroad has the cost of processing included in the purchase price. Should you wish to have any of this film processed at a Kodak Laboratory in the United States, it will be done at no additional charge.*

- *Some countries have strict import regulations affecting color film and it is the customs officers of these nations who may object to your entry with large quantities of this film. It may be possible to overcome these objections by suggesting that the officer package and seal all of your film except the few rolls you plan to shoot in his country. You would then be unable to use any film from this package until you left.*

- *Color film should not be kept for long periods between exposure and processing, especially under hot, humid conditions. If your stay abroad lasts about four weeks or less, there's relatively little risk in keeping your exposed film with you and sending it in for processing upon your return home. If you plan to be away longer, make some processing arrangements with your Kodak dealer before you leave so that you can either forward film to him from wherever you'll be or, with a Kodak Processing Mailing Label, send it to a Kodak laboratory which, in turn, will send it to him. He can either hold the film for you, and perhaps send you a card every now and then to assure you that your camera is operating satisfactorily, or, if you have a fixed itinerary, return it to you abroad. If, however, you'll be moving around at a pretty rapid rate, it's inadvisable to plan on having your film returned to you en route unless you allow an extremely generous safety margin.*

- *Kodachrome Movie Film is available nearly everywhere in the world. There are Kodak Processing Laboratories in many countries, but they cannot send your processed film to you at a United States address or at an address in any country but their own without some special arrangements being made.*

MOVIES EN ROUTE

Once you actually reach wherever it is that you're going abroad, there's usually a seemingly endless supply of prospective subject matter for your movie camera. But the enjoyable business of getting there often presents some equally engaging movie material. Keeping your camera at hand may turn out to be very much worth while.

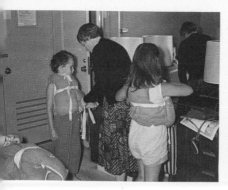

Chapter XIV

Special Techniques

Movie Tricks

A home-movie camera has more potential tricks in it than a magician's derby. An entire book might be written on this subject alone. In fact, several have. Generally, the more complex and versatile a camera is, the greater the range of legerdemain it is capable of producing, but even the simplest cameras, without single-framing provisions, slow-motion speeds, and built-in masking devices, can create remarkable effects.

One of the easiest stunts is to make people disappear. Starting with the camera on a firm support, photograph part of an activity and then, cautioning everyone in it to freeze, stop the camera. Hustle one of your subjects out of the picture, make no other changes, and begin shooting again. When you project the film, it will seem as if there's been a complete vanishing act.

A variation on this technique, one widely employed in silent movie comedies, is to have one person appear to transform himself into another. This is generally accomplished with the aid of a large tree. Someone walks right up to and behind the tree. You immediately cease shooting when most of his body becomes hidden by the tree. Then whisk him out of this location and stage someone else behind the tree. As you start shooting once more, this actor should stride out briskly, moving in the same direction as the previous participant. In your projected movie, the transformation will seem instantaneous.

Another application employs the services of the neighborhood small fry, the more of them the better. Place a large box or barrel in the middle of your scene and have one child climb out of it and walk away. Stop shooting and put another child into the box. Photograph the same action again. You can keep this up endlessly, and the box, in your film, will seem to yield an army of moppets. If you wish, you can work the trick in reverse by having the kids climb into the box. After about six or eight have done so, direct the next few to do a good deal of squirming around as they get inside, so that the box seems to be extremely crowded. When the final child walks up to the box, instead of having him get in, let him push it over, straining manfully, of course. Out might march a small dog or kitten.

Another wondrous trick is to have divers come zooming out of the water onto a diving board or boys appear to jump heights that are beyond the capabilities of Olympians. This can be managed by holding the camera upside down while you photograph a diver or a boy leaping *off* a fence. Then, after processing, the section of film should be cut out of the reel, turned top to bottom, and spliced back in. This reverses the action. With 8mm film, to keep the perforations on the correct side, it's necessary not only to turn the film top to bottom but flop it over as well. This, however, may make it necessary to refocus the projector slightly during this scene and will cause any lettering in the picture to appear backwards.

With any camera capable of single-framing, you can easily create the illusion of a hopped-up world gone mad. Simply plant the camera on a tripod or Kodak Flexiclamp and shoot some activity as a string of single frames, one right after the other, just as quickly as you can make them. The result will be a pace wild enough to make even the Keystone Cops dizzy.

As a sure antidote to apathetic audiences, treat them to a scene in which someone washing a car turn around, notices the camera, picks up his bucket of water, and hurls its contents directly at the lens. The trick is to keep the camera behind a sheet of glass during the shooting.

With a little carpentry, you can also provide wings for your movie camera. First, cut a piece of scrap wood to about the same size as the bottom of your camera. Drill a hole in it large enough for the tripod screw and countersink an area on the bottom so that the tripod screw can get through to the camera to fasten it to the wood. Next, attach this piece of wood to a five foot length of 2-by-4. For the actual shooting, start by

When a gray-coated boy runs behind a tree and turns into a red-coated girl, that's a good trick. It's also a rather easy one. With the camera on a tripod, stop shooting as soon as the boy is hidden. Replace him with the girl and begin filming again just as she starts to run out and be visible.

Obviously there's room in the barrel for only one child. To try convincing your audience this isn't so, mount your camera on a tripod and stop shooting after each child emerges. Then put another child in. For utmost realism, have the outside kids hold still whenever you stop the camera.

holding the entire apparatus steady and locking the camera button into the "on" position. Then, lift the 2-by-4 slowly and swing it in any direction you wish. The movies obtained will give the impression that gravity has lost all control of the camera. For best results, use a wide-angle lens or lens converter.

Fades

A fade-out at the end of a scene makes the picture become gradually dimmer until the screen is left entirely darkened. It's a neat way of indicating the close of a day in your movie story or the end of the film itself, or even of just a certain activity.

Really good outdoor fades can be produced only with cameras that employ an iris diaphragm to vary the size of the lens opening. The Brownie Movie Cameras and several other types use a rotating wheel with holes of various sizes in it that turns in front of the lens. Although these cameras cannot make a satisfactory fade outdoors, they can produce one indoors.

To fade-out an outdoor scene, slowly turn the collar that sets

With a camera having an iris diaphragm, a fade-out such as this one can be performed by slowly turning the lens opening collar to the smallest opening while you continue to shoot. Once you've reached the smallest opening, place one hand over the lens and shoot for another second or two.

the lens opening toward the smallest aperture while you are shooting. This gradually reduces the amount of light reaching the film. After you reach the smallest opening, cover the lens with your hand and keep shooting for a second. It's easiest to accomplish this, of course, when your camera is sitting on a tripod, but with practice and a little dexterity the trick can be performed under hand-held operating conditions. With diaphragm-type lenses this same system applies indoors.

There is another method, though, that can be used indoors with any kind of camera. Have someone take a pair of large cards, a foot square or bigger, and slowly move them in front of the photoflood lamps on your light bar while you keep operating the camera. This accomplishes the same purpose.

Fade-ins to begin a movie or some portion of a movie are achieved by reversing the fade-out technique.

Extreme Close-Ups

The nearer the distance from camera to subject, the larger the subject appears. Occasionally, being able to shoot at extremely close range is an invaluable asset, especially if your interests run to horticulture, scale model railroads, or any other field in which tiny detail is of vast importance. Every camera, though, whether its lens be of the focusing or fixed focus type, can approach only so near to a subject. Past this close-focusing limit — and it varies from one type of lens to another — the subject will photograph increasingly fuzzy and indistinct.

The close-focusing limit can be moved closer by the use of Kodak Portra Lenses. These optical units, designed to be mounted like filters over the camera lens, are available in three powers, 1+, 2+, and 3+. The 3+ Portra Lens permits the shortest camera-to-subject distance, closer than 8 inches on some cameras. Like filters, Portra Lenses should be requested by series number and must be held with an adapter ring.

Focusing-type lenses on many 8mm and 16mm cameras can be adjusted to photograph subjects only 12 inches away. At this range, the lens "sees" an area only about 3 by 4 inches. With cameras capable of such extreme close-up shooting, the 1+ and 2+ Portra Lenses offer relatively slight advantage. The 3+ Portra Lens, however, allows camera-to-subject distances ranging from about 7½ inches to 13 inches, depending upon the focus setting of the camera lens.

But fixed-focus lenses on cameras, such as those of the Brownie Movie series, permit you to shoot no closer to a subject than 3½ feet at a lens setting of 8. At this distance, the lens "sees" an area about 12 by 15 inches. A 1+ Portra Lens shifts the near limit to about 33 inches; a 2+, to 18; and a 3+, to 12. Portra Lenses, however, must be removed from the camera when photographing more distant subjects.

When making movies with a Portra Lens, the range of sharpness is extremely narrow and, when you have a 3+, it is virtually non-existent. Actual distance measurements must be made. Estimates aren't accurate enough.

DATA ON KODAK PORTRA LENSES WITH FIXED-FOCUS 8mm CAMERAS

	Range of Sharpness in Inches At Lens Setting of 8 (f/8)		Area Covered by Lens in Inches At Lens Setting of 8 (f/8)	
	From	To	Near	Far
Portra 1+	23	60	5½x7	15x20
Portra 2+	14	24½	3½x4¾	6⅛x8¼
Portra 3+	10¼	15¼	2¾x3⅝	3⅞x5⅛

But there's an even greater complication to extreme close-up shooting. On most movie cameras, the viewfinder is a couple of inches above the camera lens and therefore doesn't see exactly the same area as the film sees. At normal shooting distances, this variance is so inconsequential that it can be entirely ignored. Only at about three feet and closer does it become necessary to compensate for this parallax effect. Extremely close ranges, though, create a severe parallax problem. At 12 inches, only about the bottom half of the area visible through the finder appears in the movie frame. The remainder of the picture is below the area seen through the finder.

This makes it quite desirable to have a device that not only shows the correct camera-to-subject distance for a Portra Lens

COLLECTORS' ITEMS

When small, colorful flowers fill large movie screens, something special usually happens. Audiences gasp. The gardener is filled with a new pride in his and nature's accomplishment. A great deal of footage of a garden as a whole is bland movie fare, but when you get in close, really close, the bright cameos you capture on film will be an ample reward for the effort.

but one that marks off the exact area the camera lens sees, so that viewfinding becomes unnecessary. If this sounds like a description of a titler, it's more than merely coincidental. A titler does all this and makes titles, too. In most titlers, a Portra Lens or a similar close-up lens is built in. Generally, you can use only this one lens and only one shooting distance, but, in most cases, it's a convenient and very close one. To all but a few moviemakers, the advantages of having an all-in-one device for extreme close-ups far outweighs this slight inflexibility.

To attain the utmost in variety for extreme close-up shooting, it's essential to have a set of focal frames, each of which marks off the camera-to-subject distance and the field of view for a certain Portra Lens. These can either be ordered from a camera shop or homemade.

DATA ON KODAK PORTRA LENSES FOR 8mm CAMERAS
with focusing 13mm lenses

Camera Focus Scale Setting in Feet	Portra Lens 2+		Portra Lens 3+	
	Portra Lens-to-Subject Distance in Inches	Area Covered By Lens in Inches	Portra Lens-to-Subject Distance in Inches	Area Covered By Lens in Inches
INF.	$19\frac{1}{2}$	$5 \times 6\frac{3}{4}$	13	$3\frac{3}{8} \times 4\frac{1}{2}$
50	$19\frac{1}{8}$	$4\frac{7}{8} \times 6\frac{1}{2}$	$12\frac{7}{8}$	$3\frac{3}{8} \times 4\frac{3}{8}$
25	$18\frac{1}{2}$	$4\frac{3}{4} \times 6\frac{3}{8}$	$12\frac{1}{2}$	$3\frac{1}{4} \times 4\frac{3}{8}$
15	$17\frac{3}{4}$	$4\frac{5}{8} \times 6\frac{1}{8}$	$12\frac{1}{4}$	$3\frac{1}{4} \times 4\frac{1}{4}$
10	$16\frac{7}{8}$	$4\frac{3}{8} \times 5\frac{7}{8}$	$11\frac{7}{8}$	$3\frac{1}{8} \times 4\frac{1}{8}$
8	$16\frac{3}{8}$	$4\frac{1}{4} \times 5\frac{5}{8}$	$11\frac{1}{2}$	3×4
6	$15\frac{1}{2}$	$4 \times 5\frac{3}{8}$	$11\frac{1}{8}$	$2\frac{7}{8} \times 3\frac{7}{8}$
4	14	$3\frac{5}{8} \times 4\frac{7}{8}$	$10\frac{3}{8}$	$2\frac{5}{8} \times 3\frac{1}{2}$
3	$12\frac{5}{8}$	$3\frac{1}{4} \times 4\frac{3}{8}$	$9\frac{1}{2}$	$2\frac{1}{2} \times 3\frac{3}{8}$
2	$10\frac{1}{2}$	$2\frac{3}{4} \times 3\frac{5}{8}$	$8\frac{1}{4}$	$2\frac{1}{4} \times 3$

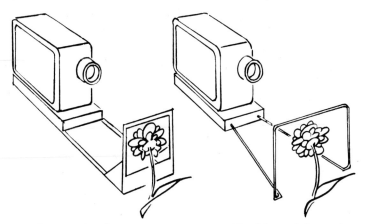

Titler in use for close-ups.   *Focal frame being used.*

DATA ON KODAK PORTRA LENSES FOR 16mm CAMERAS
with focusing 25mm lenses

Camera Focus Scale Setting in Feet	Portra Lens 2+		Portra Lens 3+	
	Portra Lens-to-Subject Distance in Inches	Area Covered By Lens in Inches	Portra Lens-to-Subject Distance in Inches	Area Covered By Lens in Inches
INF.	$19\frac{1}{2}$	$5\frac{5}{8}$x$7\frac{1}{2}$	13	$3\frac{3}{4}$x5
50	$19\frac{1}{8}$	$5\frac{3}{8}$x$7\frac{1}{4}$	$12\frac{7}{8}$	$3\frac{5}{8}$x$4\frac{7}{8}$
25	$18\frac{1}{2}$	$5\frac{1}{4}$x7	$12\frac{1}{2}$	$3\frac{1}{2}$x$4\frac{3}{4}$
15	$17\frac{3}{4}$	5x$6\frac{3}{4}$	$12\frac{1}{4}$	$3\frac{1}{2}$x$4\frac{5}{8}$
10	$16\frac{7}{8}$	$4\frac{3}{4}$x$6\frac{3}{8}$	$11\frac{7}{8}$	$3\frac{3}{8}$x$4\frac{1}{2}$
8	$16\frac{3}{8}$	$4\frac{5}{8}$x$6\frac{1}{4}$	$11\frac{1}{2}$	$3\frac{1}{4}$x$4\frac{3}{8}$
6	$15\frac{1}{2}$	$4\frac{3}{8}$x$5\frac{7}{8}$	$11\frac{1}{8}$	$3\frac{1}{8}$x$4\frac{1}{8}$
4	14	4x$5\frac{3}{8}$	$10\frac{3}{8}$	$2\frac{7}{8}$x$3\frac{7}{8}$
3	$12\frac{5}{8}$	$3\frac{1}{2}$x$4\frac{5}{8}$	$9\frac{1}{2}$	$2\frac{3}{4}$x$3\frac{5}{8}$
2	$10\frac{1}{2}$	3x4	$8\frac{1}{4}$	$2\frac{3}{8}$x$3\frac{1}{4}$

Animation

A girl in a movie jumps rope, and her action seems smooth and continuous. Examine the reel of film, though, and you see a long string of individual pictures like tiny color snapshots. In each of them, the girl's position is slightly different because she's moved somewhat in the intervals between the pictures.

The only major difference between this sort of ordinary movie action and animated movies is that the subject matter in animation isn't inherently capable of motion. It's necessary for you, then, to shoot a single frame of the subject; change its position very slightly and shoot another single frame.

As far as making single-frame exposures is concerned, nearly all 16mm cameras and many 8mm cameras have provisions for

The letters are added to the background picture one at a time and, with the camera fixed in position, two or three frames are exposed at each addition. When projected, the title seems to write itself.

Place a toy car on a map at the same place where you started a trip. Shoot one frame. Move the car slightly along your route and shoot another. Draw a red line behind the car to show the route. When the film is projected, the car seems to move by its own power.

doing this. On most of them, exposing a frame at a time is achieved by pressing the camera button in the direction opposite to the one in which you press it for ordinary movies. Single framing can be performed, though, even with cameras like those in the Brownie Movie series which aren't specifically designed to do it. By merely flicking the button lightly with the tip of your finger, you'll generally be able to expose only one or two frames at a time.

By animation, you can produce a title that seems to write itself. Start with a sheet of solid-color poster paper spread on the floor and a set of wooden letters. Mount your camera on a tripod, a requirement for all animation work, and point it down at the paper. For illumination, use your light bar. The title might be "Gerry's Baby Days." First, shoot one or two seconds' worth of the plain sheet of colored paper, as you would an ordinary movie. Then, lay the "G" on it and expose two frames. Add the second letter and shoot two more frames. Just continue this until the entire title is down. Then make about three seconds of ordinary movies of the complete title and, when projected, the words will spell out quite magically.

To title a movie of a motor trip, you could show a toy car covering the route on a road map. Again, begin by placing the map on the floor and setting up your camera and lights. Shoot about two seconds of regular movies of the map alone, preferably with your starting point at the very edge of the picture. Then put the car at the starting point and shoot one frame. Advance it slightly along your route and shoot another. In the projected scene, the car will appear to travel along under its own power. You can add a little extra fun by having it seem to bump along. For one frame, tip the front of the car up slightly by placing something under it. For the next, move it forward a little and this time prop up its back end.

For single-framing, be sure that the camera is set at 16 frames per second and that you use a lens opening one full setting *smaller* than you normally would for the distance from lights to subject. For example, if you were shooting at a range of three feet with two photofloods, the exposure table in the film instructions would recommend a setting of 8 for Kodachrome Film, Type A; in animation shots, use 11 instead.

Chapter XV

Movie Cameras and Movie Film

Camera Maintenance

A movie camera, like a camel, will go a long way with very little attention. The few spots that should be checked from time to time are:

THE LENS: If there are any dirt or fingerprints on the lens, wipe the surface gently with either a lens tissue or a clean, soft, lintless cloth. By wrapping your cleaning material around a wooden matchstick, you will be able to get at the edges. Removable lenses should be unscrewed to allow occasional cleaning of the rear face.

THE GATE: Any dirt, hair, or scraps of film that adhere to the gate can create dark marks around the edges of your movies and, perhaps, scratch them. Consult your camera instruction booklet for the correct method of removing the pressure plate. When you have it out of the camera, wipe both it and the aperture plate with a slightly moist cloth and polish them dry with a soft, lintless cloth. Do not scrape either surface with any metallic object.

THE SPRING MOTOR: Check your camera manual to find out if, when you put an empty camera away, the motor should be run down or fully wound.

Don't oil any part of your camera without first checking your instruction booklet. Many movie cameras are entirely prelubricated and never need oiling. Incorrect or unnecessary oiling can spoil your movies.

Consult your camera dealer about any repairs that you think may be required. Take a recent roll of your movies along if they seem adversely affected by improper functioning.

Different Types of Cameras

The price, usefulness, and performance of a home movie camera depend to a very great extent on its own basic characteristics. Listed below are some of these camera features along with a few of their functional implications. You may find this helpful in deciding what type of camera you should recommend to a friend, in further acquainting you with the potentialities of your own camera, or in selecting a new camera for yourself.

ROLL FILM VS MAGAZINE LOADING

Magazine loading is almost instantaneous, a boon to those whose manual equipment includes more than the normal quota of thumbs. In exchange for this convenience, though, you will generally have to pay a higher price for a magazine camera than a roll-film type of comparable quality. Magazine loads of film are also slightly more costly, the premium being approximately 25 percent over the roll-film price. With a magazine camera, you can shift from one kind of film to another even though both loads are only partially exposed. Part of this feature can be enjoyed with a roll-film camera by doing all color shooting on Type A film and, in daylight, using a Kodak Daylight Filter for Kodak Type A Color Films (No. 85).

INTERCHANGEABLE LENSES VS CONVERTIBLE LENSES

In some movie cameras, the lens can be entirely removed and interchanged with telephoto and wide-angle lenses. In other cameras, the lens is permanently mounted, but units called "converters" are available which, when fastened over the camera lens, adapt it so that it acts like a telephoto or a wide-angle lens. Converters are less costly than completely interchangeable lenses. Their optical quality is slightly inferior, but this difference would be important only to rather critical moviemakers. Converters, however, are manufactured in only a limited range of focal lengths, while the variety of interchangeable lenses for 8mm and 16mm cameras is extremely great.

SINGLE LENS VS LENS TURRET

Turret-lens cameras permit immediate switching from a lens of one focal length to a lens of another. Even when sold with only a single lens included in the basic price (a common practice), they are, however, somewhat more costly than a comparable one lens camera. Many single lens cameras have lenses that unscrew and can be replaced by other lenses of different focal lengths. This transformation cannot be achieved as quickly as on a turret camera and sometimes requires that an adapter be placed over the camera viewfinder to outline the area covered by the new lens. If the camera lens does not unscrew, chances are that wide-angle and telephoto converters are made which can be attached to it.

8MM VS 16MM

Each 16mm movie frame has about four times the area of each 8mm movie frame. This probably suggests two of the major differences between them. First, four minutes' worth of 8mm movies costs less than four minutes' worth of 16mm movies, not quite one-fourth as much but about one-third. Also, since each 16mm frame is much larger than each 8mm frame, it can be projected to a larger screen size. As long as you plan to restrict your showings to home and home-movie screens (most of them are 40 inches wide), 8mm will be entirely satisfactory. If, though, you may wish to exhibit your handiwork to large audiences on larger screens, 16mm is an absolute necessity. You'll also find that, in addition to 8mm film being less costly than 16mm, 8mm cameras and projectors will also carry lower price tags than comparable 16mm equipment. A wider variety of different kinds of film is available in the larger size and it is relatively easy to add sound at any time to 16mm films. This simply requires the addition of a magnetic stripe to the edge of the film and then the recording of commentary or background music while running the movie on a special magnetic-optical type of projector.

MAXIMUM LENS OPENING

The larger the maximum opening of a lens, the less light needed on a subject for moviemaking. To illustrate, with a two-lamp movie light bar and Kodachrome Film, Type A, in your camera, you can shoot from as far away as 9 feet if your lens is rated at $f/2.8$ and wide open. With an $f/2$ lens wide open, however, you can retreat to 12½ feet, since it will permit twice as much illumination to reach the film. If lenses are of approximately equal optical quality, the one with the larger maximum opening will nearly always be more expensive.

Most movies, both outdoor and indoor, are shot at small and medium lens openings like 8 ($f/8$) and 5.6 ($f/5.6$). At these settings, fixed-focus lenses have a wide enough range of sharpness to permit close-ups as well as medium and long shots. At larger openings, though, the near limit of sharp focus will be 6 feet or more, making real close-ups impossible unless you have a Kodak Portra Lens or other special equipment. With a focusing lens, close-ups can be made at any lens setting merely by adjusting the focus for the camera-to-subject distance. This also shifts the entire range of sharpness. For example, when an 8mm camera with a fixed-focus lens is set at 8 ($f/8$), everything from 3½ feet to infinity will turn out sharp, and anything closer than 3½ feet will be fuzzy. With a focusing lens set at 8 ($f/8$) and focused at 3½ feet, everything from 2 feet to 6 feet will be sharp. Generally, cameras with fixed-focus lenses are less costly than those supplied with focusing lenses, but if the ability to shoot close-ups under all kinds of lighting conditions is important, a focusing lens will be essential.

Black-and-White Films

Black-and-white home movie films have steadily decreased in popularity as the gap between their cost and the cost of color films has narrowed. Right now, Kodachrome Film is only about half-again more expensive than comparable black-and-white materials. Understandably, then, most people prefer color. Largely because of this, Kodak black-and-white home movie films are now available only in 16mm loads.

There are certain special situations, though, in which black-and-white films may turn out to be invaluable. Predictably, these are situations in which the use of color film is just about impossible, usually because the existing light is too dim for color shooting and a light bar would not be of any help.

Kodak Tri-X Reversal Film is ten times as sensitive to tungsten illumination as Kodachrome Film, Type A. It permits you to make good movies, albeit black-and-white movies, when there is only one-tenth as much natural, existing light as you'd need for Kodachrome.

Tri-X is ideal for moviemaking in sports arenas and at night-

lighted athletic fields. It can be used at amateur theatrical events
and in churches. Best of all, if you have to make a guess as to
the lens setting, either because you don't have a meter or because the location is one in which a meter would be useless,
Tri-X can tolerate moderate errors in exposure and still produce first-rate movies.

Tri-X should be considered primarily as a film for shooting
by rather dim existing light. Kodak Plus-X Film is an all-round,
outdoor-indoor black-and-white material. The recommended
outdoor lens setting for Plus-X Film in bright sunlight with a
camera speed of 16 frames-per-second is 16.

EXPOSURE INDEXES—KODAK BLACK-AND-WHITE REVERSAL MOVIE FILMS

Film	Daylight	Tungsten
Tri-X	200	160
Plus-X	50	40

Filters

The roster of filters for color moviemaking is an extremely
exclusive one, consisting of merely three. By all odds the most
significant of the trio is the Kodak Daylight Filter for Kodak
Type A Color Films (No. 85). This unit makes it possible to use
one kind of color film, Type A, for all your moviemaking. Outdoors, you simply slip the filter over the camera lens and use
the same settings as you would for Kodachrome Film, Daylight Type.

The Kodak Skylight Filter (No. 1A) is an extremely pale-
pink "monocle" applicable outdoors for reducing the bother-
some bluishness in movies made under cloudy or shady conditions. It also lessens the blue haze that often shrouds aerial
films and movies of mountain scenery.

The Kodak Photoflood Filter for Kodak Daylight Type Color
Films (No. 80B) operates in reverse of the Daylight Filter since

it permits the use of Daylight Type film with photofloods. It is recommended only as a makeshift, though, because it does not produce as satisfactory color rendition as Type A film and because it requires a lens opening that is a complete setting *larger* than Type A.

The Kodak Pola-Screen, although not a true filter, acts like a rather unusual one. When placed over a camera lens to photograph a scene lighted from the side, it can darken the sky to a dramatic, nearly purplish-blue; penetrate haze; and reduce undesirable reflections without affecting any of the other colors. As you observe a side-lighted scene through a Pola-Screen and rotate it slowly, you'll see that there is a certain angle at which it will have the greatest sky-darkening affect. It can then be mounted over the camera lens and turned to this angle. When the Pola-Screen is used at its maximum polarizing position, the lens opening must be two full settings *larger* than without a Pola-Screen. For example, on a bright sunny day with Kodachrome Film, Daylight Type, the normal setting would be 8; with a Pola-Screen, it must be 4. When you are concentrating your camera primarily upon the activities of nearby people, a Pola-Screen is not only difficult to use but rather negligible in results; however, for scenic footage, it offers some unique and often very desirable dividends.

Additional information on this subject appears in the Kodak Data Book, *Filters and Pola-Screens,* sold by many Kodak dealers.

Caring for Your Film

The arch-foes of unprocessed movie film are high temperature and high humidity. An excess of either can garble the colors produced by color film and alter the exposure requirements of any film, black-and-white or color.

The humidity menace is almost entirely hobbled by the type of packaging in which Kodak supplies its movie films. All magazine loads, both 8mm and 16mm, are sealed in *water-vapor-tight* envelopes of foil and plastic; rolls come in cans sealed with *water-vapor-resistant* tape. In most areas of North America, both forms of packing are proof against humidity, but, if any film in vapor-resistant containers must be stored for a week or longer in some locality commonly having relative humidities of 70 percent or greater, the factory-applied tape should be reinforced with an additional layer of ordinary adhesive tape.

Under any circumstances, the original package shouldn't be broken until you are ready to load the film into your camera.

Temperature troubles can be avoided by storing film in some part of your home not likely to become much warmer than 70 degrees. If you plan to keep any film for longer than four weeks, especially in hot summer months, place the unopened package on the bottom shelf of your refrigerator. Rolls of movie film should be sealed in a dry, rubber-sealed jar to protect them from the high humidity level. Remove the film from the refrigerator an hour or two in advance of use so that it may reach outside temperature.

Once you have loaded a roll or magazine of film into your camera, make sure, then, that the camera isn't subjected to extremes of either heat or humidity or both. Never leave it on the rear deck, in the glove compartment, or in the trunk of an automobile.

The briefer the length of time a roll of film remains in your camera, the better. If you expose a dozen feet of film at one time and then finish the roll several months later, chances are that there will be a noticeable difference in color quality between the two sections. Not only should a roll or magazine of film be exposed over a fairly brief period of time, but the film should be processed as soon as possible after being taken from the camera.

Processed film is vulnerable to not only heat and humidity but to strong light as well. Light can affect the dyes which form the color in color movies. Keep your films out of attics and basements and away from heating pipes. Moisture is an especial hazard since it may cause fungus growths on the film. A 200-foot reel and reel can for 8mm movies cost a little more than a dollar and offer an inexpensive way of protecting irreplaceable films from light.

Should any finger marks or dirt become attached to your movies, the most effective means of cleaning them is by passing the film lightly through a pad of cotton nearly saturated with Kodak Movie Film Cleaner (with Lubricant).

Chapter XVI

Projection

Screens

A matte projection screen is not likely to provide quite as brilliant a picture as a beaded screen, but since its surface is smoother, the picture on it can be viewed from farther to the side. With a beaded screen, all of your audience should be seated inside an arc of forty degrees, measured from the center of the screen; with a matte surface, the angle can be sixty degrees.

Any screen should be erected in the darkest possible location and be high enough so that it is visible to the viewers in the rear row. It is especially important that no stray light strike a beaded screen from behind the audience. If you have a matte screen, make certain that there's no light near it during a showing.

The screen must be perpendicular to the projector. If it isn't, the picture image will stretch into a distorted form. This should be checked when you set up the screen and projector rather than after your audience is at hand.

Screens generally demand very little special maintenance. The beaded type may tend to become dusty after a while, due to the coarseness of its surface. Specific cleaning instructions will probably be packed with your screen. In general, dusting should be performed with an extremely soft brush of the kind used on babies' hair. Stiff bristles may remove the beaded finish. If a beaded screen becomes spotted, consult either the screen instructions or the screen manufacturer. Not all beaded screens can be washed.

Dust can be removed from a matte surface also with a soft brush. Most matte screens may be cleaned with a damp cloth.

185

PROJECTION DATA—MATTE AND BEADED SCREENS

Projector	Lens	Lamp Wattage	Matte Screen		Beaded Screen	
			Approximate Picture Width	Approximate Screen Distance	Approximate Picture Width	Approximate Screen Distance
8mm	¾-inch f/1.6	300	30 inches	11 feet	32 inches	11½ feet
		500	40 inches	15 feet	44 inches	15½ feet
	1-inch f/1.6	300	30 inches	15 feet	32 inches	15½ feet
		500	40 inches	20 feet	44 inches	21 feet
		750	3½ feet	22 feet	4 feet	23 feet
		1000	4 feet	25 feet	4½ feet	25 feet
16mm	2-inch f/1.6	300	5 feet	26 feet	5 feet	27 feet
		500	6 feet	32 feet	6½ feet	34 feet
		750	7 feet	36 feet	7¼ feet	38 feet
		1000	8 feet	42 feet	8½ feet	45 feet

Silent Projectors

A movie projector should be situated far enough away from the screen so that, if at all possible, its picture fills the entire screen area. It should also be high enough for its beam to clear the heads of the audience. If a projector is considerably beneath screen level, distortion will probably occur.

Always have your projector ready to go before your audience files in. Start by cleaning its lens gently with a lens tissue or a soft, relatively lint-free cloth. Every once in a while, the projector's film gate — the place at which each frame is actually projected — needs to be wiped, too. Your instruction booklet will show how.

When you connect your projector to an electrical outlet, wind its cord several turns around the leg of the table on which it is sitting. If anyone should then accidentally trip over the cord in the darkness, the projector won't be seriously damaged. Thread the projector and run some film through. This gives you an opportunity to focus and to level. Once you've done both, stop the projector and reverse the film until you reach the very beginning of the reel. Stop it again, and you're all prepared to launch a showing without any pause or irritating delay.

When you project more than one reel, don't do any rewinding until all have been projected. With rented films, the company from which you rent may prefer that you not rewind at all. At the end of a showing, turn the projection lamp off, but let the motor continue running for a few minutes to cool the projector.

On the new prelubricated projectors, maintenance may amount to no more than keeping the lens and film gate clean. Certainly, before applying oil to any part of a projector, consult the instruction booklet. To a prelubricated machine, oiling can be quite harmful, and to one that isn't prelubricated, incorrect application can be equally damaging.

Once your projection lamp begins to blacken, it should be replaced even though it may still seem to provide a fairly considerable amount of illumination.

Should your projector not operate correctly and you cannot, yourself, diagnose the difficulty, return it to your dealer. He may be able to correct the problem or will send it to either the manufacturer's service department or some reliable independent organization.

Sound Projection

Sound projection has some unique wrinkles. One of the most important is that you should warm up the amplifier before you start running a film. If you commence with a cold amplifier and adjust the volume to suit it, when the system does warm up it will bang out a thunderous "Anvil Chorus" on your eardrums.

When setting up screen and projector, the speaker should be located fairly near the screen and at screen level. Either keep it entirely away from any walls or place it in a corner. Test the sound system and adjust the volume at the same time as you attend to the focus and leveling. When your audience enters, then, you can immediately show movies without any tedious dial twiddling.

Amplifier tubes ought to be tested twice a year and defective ones replaced. If both your projection lamp and amplifier ever cut out, check the power supply. If only the sound fails, investigate the speaker cord at the jack that connects it to the amplifier. Trace any amplifier difficulties as directed in your projector instruction booklet.

Sound films are usually made at 24 frames per second rather than 16, and the projector must be operated at higher speed.

Adding Sound to Your Movies

Only the most taciturn individual ever has a truly silent movie. Nearly every showing of every film is accompanied by some sort of oral commentary, usually supplied by its creator. Orally, of course, is the very easiest way of adding sound.

Background music via phonograph or tape recordings is an added refinement. Although it's quite desirable to have the music originate from alongside the screen, this usually turns out to be a rather inconvenient location, at least to whomever is operating the projector. If, in your arsenal of audio equipment, you have an extension speaker, you might locate this up front, but keep the remainder of the paraphernalia alongside the projector. For an added touch, especially if you're an electrical gadgeteer, a microphone could be wired into the circuit so that your comments will also emanate from the speaker.

One of the great obstacles in this sort of hookup is the length of the recordings. While a certain piece of music may be entirely appropriate to scenes of skiers whipping over a slope, it's probably out of character for, say, a late-evening party at the ski lodge. If you have the luxury of two turntables, you can overcome a good bit of this problem by switching from one to another, but a tape recorder will solve it a great deal more conveniently.

With a recorder and a phonograph, you can prepare a special tape to accompany the showing of any of your films. A certain musical selection may be made to last only as long as the scenes it fits. You can even add sound effects. Exact synchronization isn't at all essential. Your camera dealer can probably advise you of some sources of sound effects recordings.

For a zany touch, a movie-plus-taped-sound can be assembled so that all of the noises are intentionally ridiculous. A scene showing a steamship's great whistle might be accompanied by a fifelike trill; a view of a great waterfall, by a drip-drip-drip from the kitchen faucet.

The ultimate achievement is the addition of a complete sound track directly on a 16mm movie. With present magnetic sound equipment it has become easy, economical, and satisfactory enough to be of considerable interest to schools, business concerns, church groups, television stations, civic organizations, and home-movie fans. In this system the processed film is striped along one edge with a material similar to that used on regular magnetic tape. Kodak's coating of this kind is called "Sonotrack" and is available through Kodak dealers. It can be applied in three widths, the widest for single-perforated film having no existing optical sound track; the middle-size for single perforated film having an existing optical sound track; and the narrowest for double perforated film.

Once the magnetic coating has been applied, the film can be run through a 16mm magnetic-type sound projector. While it is being projected, a very simple or a fairly complex sound track can be applied. It's possible to feed background music onto the stripe. You can add sound effects, either from a recording or through the microphone. On top of this, a vocal commentary may be transcribed. Just as with ordinary tape recording, any errors can be wiped out and corrected.

Movies that are going to have magnetic sound tracks should, preferably, be exposed at 24 frames per second since the sound, then, will have better fidelity. Sound, however, can be recorded at 16 frames per second for films shot at that camera speed.

Magnetic sound films should be edited before the addition of the striping, not only because this will turn out to be more economical but also because there is a possibility that, when a splicer is used on striped film, its steel scraper and cutter may become magnetized. Should this occur, a noticeable click will be heard through the speaker during projection every time a splice travels through the sound head.

Some film cleaners have a tendency to soften magnetic sound stripings. As a precaution, test any you are planning to use on the end of the film before applying it generally.

Index

190

S

T

V

W